COMMON SENSE

THOMAS PAINE was born in Thetford, England, in 1737, the son of a staymaker. He had little schooling and worked at a number of jobs, including tax collector, a position he lost for agitating for an increase in excisemen's pay. Persuaded by Benjamin Franklin, he emigrated to America in 1774. In 1776 he began his *American Crisis* series of thirteen pamphlets, and also published the incalculably influential *Common Sense*, which established Paine not only as a truly revolutionary thinker, but as the American Revolution's fiercest political theorist. In 1787 Paine returned to Europe, where he became involved in revolutionary politics. In England his books were burned by the public hangman. Escaping to France, Paine took part in drafting the French constitution and voted against the king's execution. He was imprisoned for a year and narrowly missed execution himself. In 1802 he returned to America and lived in New York State, poor, ill and largely despised for his extremism and so-called atheism (he was in fact a deist). Thomas Paine died in 1809. His body was exhumed by William Cobbett, and the remains were taken to England for a memorial burial. Unfortunately, the remains were subsequently lost.

ISAAC KRAMNICK was born in 1938 and educated at Harvard University, where he received a B.A. degree in 1959 and a Ph.D. in 1965, and at Peterhouse, Cambridge. He has taught at Harvard, Brandeis, Yale and Cornell, where he is now Professor of Government. He is married to Miriam Brody Kramnick and lives in Ithaca, New York. Among his publications are *Bolingbroke and His Circle*, *The Rage of Edmund Burke* and numerous articles on eighteenth century topics. He has edited William Godwin's *Enquiry Concerning Political Justice*, *The Federalist Papers* by James Madison, Alexander Hamilton and John Jay and, with Michael Foot, *The Thomas Paine Reader* for the Penguin Classics. Most recently he is the author, with Barry Sheerman, MP, of *Laski: A Life on the Left*.

THOMAS PAINE

COMMON SENSE

EDITED WITH
AN INTRODUCTION BY
ISAAC KRAMNICK

PENGUIN BOOKS

PENGUIN BOOKS

Published by the Penguin Group
Penguin Books Ltd, 27 Wrights Lane, London W8 5TZ, England
Penguin Books USA Inc., 375 Hudson Street, New York, New York 10014, USA
Penguin Books Australia Ltd, Ringwood, Victoria, Australia
Penguin Books Canada Ltd, 10 Alcorn Avenue, Toronto, Ontario, Canada M4V 3B2
Penguin Books (NZ) Ltd, 182–190 Wairau Road, Auckland 10, New Zealand

Penguin Books Ltd, Registered Offices: Harmondsworth, Middlesex, England

First published 1776
Published in Pelican Books 1976
Reprinted in Penguin American Library 1982
Reprinted in Penguin Classics 1986
15 17 19 20 18 16

Introduction copyright © Isaac Kramnick, 1976
All rights reserved

Printed in England by Clays Ltd, St Ives plc
Set in Monotype Garamond

CONTENTS

EDITOR'S INTRODUCTION

BACKGROUND TO THE AMERICAN
REVOLUTION, 1776

AMERICANS fought Englishmen on the battlefields of the new world in January 1776, even as, among themselves, they debated the nature and purpose of those battles. Nine months earlier, on 19 April 1775, General Gage, the military Governor of Massachusetts, had tried to destroy military supplies which militant colonists had been collecting at Concord, Massachusetts. Paul Revere's ride through the night warned the Middlesex farmers that Gage's troops were moving from Boston. The colonial 'minutemen' summoned from their farms battled with the English regulars at Lexington and Concord. Two months later, a bloody battle took place on a hillside outside Boston. The colonists were defeated, but it was a costly victory for the English, who suffered 1,054 casualties. The summer of 1775 had also seen a makeshift American army invade Canada and capture Montreal. By December, two American divisions had surrounded and attacked Quebec, though they failed to capture it.

However, the colonists were far from clear about what they were fighting for. Some, like John and Sam Adams of Massachusetts, and Benjamin Franklin, recently returned from England, saw the hostilities as a war of independence, an attempt by the colonies to rip themselves completely from the British Empire and to establish a free and independent nation of the thirteen colonies. Others, like John Dickinson of Philadelphia, wanted to stay within the Empire. The purpose of the war as far as he was concerned was to force Parliament to acknowledge the justice of colonial claims and to redress the long litany of grievances that had led to the present confrontation. Dickinson had, in fact, persuaded the Pennsylvania legislature to instruct its delegation to the Second Continental Congress in the fall of 1775 to vote against independence if the issue were raised. Despite the influence of militants in the colonial legislatures Dickinson's was the dominant view in January 1776. Four other middle colonies followed Pennsylvania's lead in giving specific instructions to oppose any move to independence. On the other hand, not one colony had given specific instructions that its delegates vote for a definite break with England. The best estimates are that no more than a third of the members of the Congress assembled at Philadelphia through the winter of late 1775 and early 1776 were in favor of independence.

The publication of Paine's *Common Sense* could not have been better timed. The delegates who read it on the January day it appeared in Philadelphia were, like most Americans at the time, confused and ambivalent. Tied by kinship, culture, commerce and decades of loyalty to England, they found themselves suddenly at war with His Majesty's troops. But Paine, the Englishman, had no doubt about the right course. Boldly he announced that America's purpose in these battles was to achieve complete independence, to break all ties with corrupt and tyrannical Britain.

The success of *Common Sense* was phenomenal. Benjamin Rush, whose idea it had been that Paine write it, recalled that 'it burst from the press with an effect which has rarely been produced by types and papers in any age or country'. Franklin described its effect as 'prodigious'. Americans devoured the pamphlet in the early months of 1776. According to Paine, it sold some 120,000 copies in its first three months. One biographer estimates that 500,000 copies were published that year alone.

No one will ever know the exact role of *Common Sense* in changing American opinion in favor of independence in 1776. There were, certainly, other factors at work which help account for the pronounced shift of public opinion which developed as the year wore on. News of the hiring of German troops against his own people by George III helped accelerate the movement for freedom. The very day Paine's *Common Sense* was published a copy reached Philadelphia of the King's speech to Parliament several months earlier which constituted a severe setback for the American opponents of independence. In that speech, George III had declared that 'the rebellious war' in the colonies was 'manifestly carried on for the purpose of establishing an independent empire'. Militants could now refer to this clear threat from their dreaded opponent. In the South, opinion seemed to shift dramatically toward independence when the Royal Governor of Virginia frightened the planters by calling for Negro slaves to revolt against their owners. These factors played their part, as did the intensification of suffering and war. But no single event seems to have had the catalytic effect of Paine's *Common Sense*. It captured the imagination of the colonists as had no previous pamphlet. No learned treatise, no lawyer's brief, no philosophical discourse, *Common Sense* was a blunt and direct argument written in a language that could be understood by any literate colonist, whether simple farmer or plain mechanic. Not only was it widely read, it was equally widely applauded. When, for example, a pamphlet attacking *Common Sense* was published in New York, a 'committee of mechanics' destroyed all the copies before they could be sold. Paine's piece of January 1776 was, in the assessment of the distinguished American historian Bernard Bailyn, 'the most brilliant pamphlet written during the American Revolution, and one of the most brilliant pamphlets ever written in the English language'.[1]

The balance of forces was changing. First Massachusetts informed its delegates in Philadelphia that it favored independence. April 1776 found North Carolina following suit. In May, Virginia instructed its representatives in the Continental Congress actively to propose independence. By the end of June all the colonial assemblies were in favor. Richard Henry Lee rose on behalf of Virginia on 7 June 1776 to move that 'these united colonies are, and of right ought to be, free and independent states'. John Adams seconded the motion. Opponents arguing that they 'were not yet ripe for bidding adieu to the British connection', were able to delay action for three weeks. The motion was brought up before the Congress again on 1 July. Nine colonies voted for it, Pennsylvania and South Carolina against. The Delaware delegation was tied and New York excused from voting. The following day when the final vote was taken all the delegates except New York voted for independence. Two days later, on 4 July 1776, the final draft of the Declaration of Independence was adopted.

Only ten years earlier, Benjamin Franklin had been asked by the House of Commons about 'the temper of America towards Great Britain before the year 1763'. He answered that it was the 'best in the world'. The colonists, he told the Commons,

submitted willingly to the government of the Crown, and paid, in all their courts, obedience to acts of Parliament. Numerous as the people are in the several old provinces, they cost you nothing in forts, citadels, garrisons or armies, to keep them in subjection. They were governed by this country at the expense only of a little pen, ink, and paper. They were led by a thread. They had not only a respect, but an affection, for Great Britain, for its laws, its customs and manners, and even a fondness for its fashions, that greatly increased the commerce. Natives of England were always treated with particular regard; to be an Old-England man was, of itself, a character of some respect, and gave a kind of rank among us.[2]

Few dispute Franklin's assessment. Before 1763 the relationship between America and England appears to have been satisfactory to both parties. Why, then, did this relationship so degenerate that in a mere twelve years the colonies were at war with Britain and one year later declaring their independence? What happened to the respect, affection and fondness?

Most historians begin answering these questions by citing England's new economic policies of 1763 as the beginning of the estrangement between England and the thirteen colonies. The assumption is that had the English government not in 1763 abandoned its traditional policies toward America the cosy and convenient relationship described by Franklin in 1766 would have persisted. But before turning to these policies and the diplomatic controversies they generated in the critical period between 1763 and 1775, it is important to note, Franklin's assessment notwithstanding, that all was not so harmonious in the decades before 1763. Long-term factors were at work which made the connection a less than perfect one.

Despite the surface calm there were, as Professor Jack Greene of Johns Hopkins has persuasively argued, important structural changes taking place both in the colonies and in Britain during the century from 1660 to 1760 which contributed to the uneasiness of their relationship and which provided the preconditions for the American Revolution.[3] By 1750, for example, most of the colonies had virtually all the requisites of self-governing states. In each colony an effective local *élite* dominated political and social life. In addition, each of the colonies possessed autonomous local centers of administration and political authority. Particularly important in this sphere were the popularly elected lower houses of assembly in each colony. Indeed, in the century before the Revolution colonial Americans participated in the political process much more extensively than did their British cousins.

During this same period the size and wealth of the colonies increased tremendously, in terms of population as well as the amount of productive and settled land. By 1760 not only were the colonies capable of governing themselves but to a great extent they were in fact doing so, keeping order and providing the security within which merchants and planters prospered. British authority in the colonies before 1760 was weak and ineffective. Not the least of the problems was communication. It was not until 1755 that a scheduled run of packet-boats between Britain and the colonies was organized, and before the French and Indian War, which began in the mid-1750s, there was but a handful of regular English troops in the colonies.

While the British presence in the colonies was weak throughout the eighteenth century, and while its power and influence over the Americans was by no means dominant and certainly not oppressive, the colonies, on the other hand, had become of vital importance to the British economy. In 1700 their population was 257,060, rising dramatically in sixty years to 1,593,625. This fast-growing population bought large amounts of British manufactured products while in turn supplying the mother country with inexpensive raw materials. The colonies thus played a critical part in English trade, accounting in 1772–3 for 36 per cent of the total volume of English imports and 37 per cent of the total volume of English exports. Far from the colonies being weak and dependent subsidiaries of Britain, it would appear that the British economy was fast becoming dependent on the colonies.

It is this above all else which accounts for the decisive political events of the 1760s. English officials saw on the one hand the rapid growth and development of colonial economic and political institutions and on the other the importance of these colonies for the prosperity and power of England. Fearful of the disastrous consequences to Britain of a loss of control over the colonies, the British government sought not only to maintain but to intensify its economic and political hegemony.

In 1763 George Grenville became George III's first minister. Now the urge to solidify imperial authority in the colonies was matched by the desire to make America pay for the vast expenses of the recently concluded French and Indian War (the Seven Years' War in its European face). England had spent some £82,000,000 in the war and acquired as a result of it all of French Canada and the territory east of the Mississippi except Louisiana. It reckoned on a standing army of 10,000 men as necessary to protect this American empire, at a cost of £300,000 annually. Grenville turned to the colonies for revenue. This was only fair, his government assumed. The war and the standing army were both part of a policy to protect the colonies, after all. It was this conjunction of objectives that made 1763 so important. The short-range need to reform the financial structure of the colonial empire, victorious but impoverished by war, produced a program which at the same time answered the more deeply felt need for increased and more rigid control by Britain over the economy and politics of the colonies.

Grenville's program involved posting British naval vessels off North America and stationing a regular British army on the frontiers, as well as providing troops in support of British officials in the coastal colonies, if this proved necessary. The British government also forbade settlement west of the Appalachian Mountains, which closed off vast areas from pioneers, land speculators and fur traders. Even more onerous were three other measures taken by Grenville's ministry in 1764 and 1765. The Sugar Act imposed new duties and elaborate regulations on trade in and out of colonial ports. Many of the old provisions of the Navigation Acts, evaded for decades, were revived. Heavy taxes were imposed on goods imported to the colonies unless they were shipped by way of England. The Stamp Act levied a direct tax in the form of stamp duties on all legal documents, newspapers and advertisements, while the Quartering Act obliged colonial government to provide free supplies whenever British troops were stationed in colonial barracks.

For the colonists Grenville's policies represented a sharp break with traditional assumptions about the imperial relationship. Britain, it had long been assumed, would do nothing to hamper the free pursuit of colonial social and economic interests. Now it was interfering in a blatant and novel manner. The interests most affected – merchants by the trade restrictions, and lawyers and newspapermen by the Stamp Act – led the angry response of the colonists, triggering off the chain of events that culminated in Philadelphia in 1776. James Otis of Massachusetts, Stephen Hopkins of Rhode Island and Patrick Henry of Virginia argued that Parliament had no right to tax the colonies without their own consent. A Stamp Act Congress with delegates from nine colonies met in New York in October 1765 and issued a declaration attacking taxation without representation. This was deemed preposterous in British government circles. Lord Mansfield, Chief Justice of the King's Bench, told the House of Lords in 1766:

There can be no doubt, my Lords, but that the inhabitants of the colonies are as much represented in Parliament as the greatest part of the people of England are represented: among nine millions of whom there are eight which have no vote in electing members of Parliament ... A member of Parliament chosen for any borough represents not only the constituents and inhabitants of that particular place, but he represents ... all the other commons of this land, and the inhabitants of all the colonies and dominions of Great Britain.[4]

But the colonists did more than just issue declarations and draft petitions to King and Parliament. They boycotted English goods and they used direct action. Popular demonstrations were held, stamp tax collectors intimidated and British government property destroyed. The merchants were soon heard in London. In 1766 George III replaced Grenville with Rockingham and the great Whig magnate in turn pushed through the repeal of the Stamp Act. Public protest had seemingly turned the tide, a fact not lost on more militant forces in America. The victory was short-lived, however. Rockingham was out of office in the summer of 1766 and in the new government the Chancellor of the Exchequer, Charles Townshend, returned to Grenville's position that America was essentially subordinate to Britain and obliged to pay its keep in the Empire. In a series of acts that bear his name Townshend got Parliament to impose duties on glass, lead, tea and paper. The duties were to be collected by British officers stationed in American ports, and smugglers were to be tried without juries. Another act in 1767 suspended the New York Assembly for refusing to comply completely with provisions of the Quartering Act.

Once again the colonists reacted in anger. They feared not only what they considered to be English efforts to ruin the colonial economy but attacks on what they considered their traditional rights of self-government. Colonial assemblies, juries – nothing seemed safe any more. Pamphlets and petitions came rapidly from colonial presses. The most famous of these was John Dickinson's *Letters from a Farmer in Pennsylvania to the Inhabitants of the British Colonies.* The Townshend duties were unjust, un-English and a grave threat to the future of the colonies.

Let us consider ourselves as ... freemen ... firmly bound together by the same rights, interests, and dangers ... What have these colonies to ask, while they continue free; or what have they to dread, but insidious attempts to subvert their freedom? ... They form one political body, of which each colony is a member.[5]

Parliament had no right to tax for revenue, the colonial legislatures, Dickinson and others argued. Resolutions were passed in defense of the natural and constitutional rights of the colonies. In Massachusetts and Virginia the royal governors dissolved the legislatures which protested so loudly.

Direct action again supplemented protesting pens. Commercial boycotts of English goods spread throughout the coastal cities, often with more militant patriots policing those who failed to live up to non-importation agreements. Violence against English officials and property, sometimes by mob action, also increased. Customs boats were sunk, Officers tarred and feathered, English houses burned or destroyed. It was in response to incidents like these that the British took a step that proved catastrophic in exacerbating colonial rage. They introduced troops to compel, by force if necessary, the colonists to accept whatever laws the British deigned to hand down for their recalcitrant empire.

Garrisons had been maintained for some time in America, but primarily on the frontiers. The troops who arrived in Boston in the fall of 1768 were something new and unsettling. Their presence was grist for the militant mill of Sam Adams, who here saw proof positive of the English plot to impose tyranny on the innocent citizens of Boston. The constant tension between the English troops and the Boston mob came to a head in the events of March 1770, rather insignificant in any objective sense but destined to be of considerable symbolic importance. On 5 March 1770 an English sentry was pelted with snowballs. He called for assistance, and a crowd gathered. The soldiers were taunted; sticks, stones and epithets were thrown. Confusion ensued. Someone shouted 'fire'. The soldiers started shooting and three Americans in the crowd fell dead. The English troops were tried by a civilian jury and acquitted. But the indomitable Sam Adams still branded them 'murderers' and named the incident 'The Boston Massacre'. It was, he insisted, the first stage of the British plan to snuff out the light of liberty in the new world.

Colonial opinion was by no means solidly behind Sam Adams and his politics of radical agitation. Moderate merchant leaders of protest were, in fact, appalled and frightened by his tactics. For many of the well-to-do, Sam Adams and his mob of mechanics and debtors had become a veritable monster. It had been called into being to impress the British with the depths of public opposition to the new imperial policies. But the mob took on a life of its own and sought its own interests which were threatening to the substantial wealth and power of the ruling *élite* in the colonies. Parallel to the conflict with England, then, Americans were themselves divided in social conflict. All the talk of justice, equity and natural rights directed against the English was as easily directed against the domestic tyranny imposed on backwoods farmers and urban artisans by the powerful merchants and large landowners who dominated colonial life.

Recognizing the politicization of what they called the 'mob' and its threat to their dominance, many merchants softened in their opposition to the innovations of British policy. Better, many felt, to live with the new trade regulations than produce majority rule in the colonies at the hands of artisans and farmers. It was not at all certain, however, that the merchants could turn off their mob's protest as easily as they could mute their own. For some two years the moderate merchants seemed successful in treading the thin line between too much pressure and too much reliance on the mob. Calm prevailed from 1770 to 1772. Moderates had gained the upper hand both in England and the colonies. The Townshend duties were repealed with the exception of the duty on tea, partly as a result of the colonial boycott and partly because they increased the cost of the military establishment in America without generating much revenue. In America men of property were wary of fanning the fires of discontent. Cadwallader Colden, Lieutenant Governor of New York, noted that

all men of property are so sensible of their danger from riots and turncoats that they will not rashly be induced to enter into combinations which may promote disorder for the future, but will endeavor to promote due subordination to legal authority.[6]

Militants like Sam Adams still insisted that the only alternative to British opposition was complete independence and that, once free, America would not be governed by one particular class of men. In late 1772 and early 1773 Adams set up a network of committees of correspondence, first in Massachusetts and then in colony after colony. These committees became a powerful tool for militant action in the next few years.

If the militants were to succeed, however, they needed further repressive action on the part of the British government, and this they suffered in 1773. Facing bankruptcy, the East India Company was granted a monopoly of the tea trade in America. Tea could be purchased only from the Company; colonial importers were excluded. Fearful at the precedent and the prospect of other articles of trade being

monopolized by British interests, the colonial merchants
were thrown back into the arms of the militants, even
though they expected to dominate the alliance as they had
in the past. The merchants advocated commercial boycott,
the militants direct action, violence, tarring and feathering.
In Boston Sam Adams summoned a great meeting in
which it was decided that East India tea should not be
landed. On the night of 16 December 1773 a group of men
disguised as Indians boarded the Company's ships in
Boston Harbor and threw 342 chests of tea into the water
to the great delight of a large crowd looking on from the
shore.

It was not the Boston Tea Party itself but British reaction
to it which made the event so critical in accelerating the
rush of events to war and independence. The British
government over-reacted. In seeking to punish the colonists it used repressive force so unexpected and so intense
that it served only to produce new recruits for the militant
cause. These measures were embodied in what the colonists
immediately labeled the 'Intolerable Acts'. The port of
Boston was closed until the tea was paid for and assurances
were given that His Majesty's customs would be paid. The
Charter of Massachusetts was revoked, giving the royal
governor more power. Trials for capital offenses in Massachusetts were moved to England and the Quartering
Act was made more onerous, requiring local authorities
to find quarters for English troops within twenty-four
hours.

While few Americans spoke of Independence, division
persisted on the proper response to what most considered
the tyrannical implication of the 'Intolerable Acts'.
Suggestions were made in the spring and summer of 1774
in colony after colony that an intercolonial congress be
convened to discuss the new situation. In September
delegates from all thirteen colonies except Georgia (the

royal governor prevented the selection of delegates from that colony) met in Philadelphia at the First Continental Congress. For ten years each colony had made its own decisions about how to respond to British policy; now for the first time in American history the colonies had with their illegal congress a central policy making body. But what to do with it, was the question. The militants called on the congress to take a strong stand in defense of America's violated rights and to declare a complete boy-cott of English goods. The moderate delegates led by Joseph Galloway of Pennsylvania sought conciliation with England and proposed a redefinition of the imperial structure: some authority should be given an American legislature under the presidency of a crown-appointed official. In a close vote a slim majority of the fifty-six delegates defeated the conciliatory approach of the moderates. In its stead the congress adopted a manifesto of rights insisting that the colonists were 'entitled to life, liberty, and property and . . . had never ceded to any foreign power whatever, a right to dispose of either without their consent'.

The militants in the First Continental Congress seldom spoke directly of independence but they did succeed in pushing through an extreme measure of resistance known as the Association – an agreement that after 1 December 1774 no goods of any kind were to be imported from Britain. If this failed to bring a change of heart to His Majesty's government it was further agreed that after 10 September 1775 all exports to Britain would cease. Milit-ants saw to the enforcement of the Association and in one colony after another the proceedings of the congress were ratified by the legislative assembly. The import trade from England dropped a spectacular 97 per cent throughout the colonies in 1775 from the levels of the preceding year.

Lord North and his government would not budge,

however. They turned a deaf ear to American manifestos as well as to petitions from angry English businessmen with interests in America. By refusing to obey Parliamentary law and by setting up agencies like the Association, the colonists were in open rebellion, and rebellions had to be suppressed. 'An enemy in the bowels of a Kingdom', Solicitor General Wedderburn told the House of Commons, 'is surely to be resisted, opposed, and conquered; notwithstanding the trade that may suffer, and the fabrics that may be ruined.'[7] On 30 March 1775 Parliament responded with the Restraining Act designed to destroy the commerce of New England. Her trade was confined to Great Britain, Ireland and the British West Indies until 'the trade and commerce of His Majesty's subjects may be carried on without interruption'. While colonial militants drilled troops and gathered military supplies, Lord North, Parliament and George III were closing all avenues to conciliation.

Not all Englishmen urged repression, however. Pitt, for example, argued for the repeal of the Intolerable Acts. He warned the House of Lords:

Every motive of justice and of policy, of dignity and of prudence urges you to allay the ferment in America; by the removal of your troops from Boston, by a repeal of your Acts of Parliament, and by a display of amicable disposition towards your colonies. On the other hand, every danger and every hazard impend to deter you from perseverence in your present ruinous course.[8]

Edmund Burke urged conciliation with America in a famous speech to the House of Commons on 22 March 1775. His colleagues did not understand Americans, he insisted.

In this character of the Americans a love of freedom is the predominating feature, which marks and distinguishes the whole; and as an ardent is always a jealous affection, your colonies become suspicious, restive, and untractable, whenever they see the least attempt to wrest from them by force, or shuffle them by chicane, what they think the only advantage worth living for. This fierce spirit of liberty is stronger in the English colonies, probably, than in any people of the earth.

Less than a month before Concord and Lexington and the shots 'heard round the world', Burke argued that conciliation by North's government would probably bring the Americans back to the imperial fold.

My hold of the colonies is in the close affection which grows from common names, from kindred blood, from similar privileges, and equal protection. These are the ties which, though light as air, are as strong as links of iron. Let the colonies always keep the idea of their civil rights associated with your government; they will cling and grapple to you, and no force under heaven will be of power to tear them from their allegiance. But let it be once understood that your government may be one thing and their privileges another; that these two things may exist without any mutual relations; the cement is gone; the cohesion is loosened; and everything hastens to decay and dissolution.[9]

Impressive and useful as the support of statesmen like Pitt and Burke was to the Americans, it was to English radical circles that patriots in the colonies really looked for support. Mansfield's speech of 1766 noted with disdain the similarity in their causes. English radicals like the Reverends Price and Priestley and politicians like John Wilkes sought the reform of Parliament and the English constitution in the name of the same natural and historical rights as those to which the Americans appealed. They, too, demanded representation in Parliament for those taxed by Parliament. It came as no surprise then that in 1775 John Wilkes, by then Lord Mayor of London, strongly defended the colonists in Parliament and was soon involved with the French playwright Beaumarchais (*The Marriage of Figaro*) in a clandestine arrangement by which French aid was sent to the colonies.

Radicals in England stressed the unity between American and English grievances and predicted that should revolution occur in America they would not be far behind in the mother country. Efforts seemed afoot to set up provincial associations of English radicals to send aid to the Americans as well as to bring down the wicked tyranny that oppressed Americans and Englishmen alike. In October 1775 some colonists in Middletown, Connecticut, were speaking of 'committees of association ... forming throughout the Kingdom of Ireland and England', committees that would bring down George III. The King, meanwhile, was well aware of the existence of what he called 'traitorous correspondence, counsels and comfort of divers wicked and desperate persons within this realm'. He called upon his subjects 'to use their utmost endeavours to withstand and suppress ... rebellion, and to disclose ... all treasons and traitorous conspiracies which they shall know to be against us, our crown and dignity'.[10] The citizens of Middletown, Connecticut, notwithstanding, no supportive insurrections materialized in England. The Americans had to proceed on their own.

With the failure of radical Englishmen to come to the support of the colonists and with the failure of Parliament and King to work for an accommodation within the framework of the old Empire, more and more Americans overcame the instinctive respect and affection for Great Britain that Franklin had earlier discerned, and independence became conceivable. Americans could now speak of Britain as 'a vile imposter – an old abandoned prostitute – a robber, a murderer ... a Jezebel'.[11] The outbreak of hostilities in 1775 heightened the mood of alienation. Paine's *Common Sense* appeared in January 1776. Opinion shifted decisively to independence and the Continental

Congress acted in June and July. The thirteen colonies had become a free and independent nation. But war, as it always does, lingered on for what seemed an interminable period. Britain refused to recognize the independence of her colonies until the Peace Treaty of 1783. Two years earlier Cornwallis already knew as he surrendered to Washington at Yorktown that all was lost. As his troops laid down their arms the British general ordered melancholy tunes played by his band, according to the military etiquette of the day. Among them he asked that one particular old English nursery rhyme be played:

> If buttercups buzz
> after the bee;
> If boats were on land,
> churches on sea;
> If ponies rode men,
> and grass ate the cow;
> If cats should be chased
> into holes by the mouse;
> If mammas sold their babies
> to gypsies for half a crown;
> If summer were spring
> and the other way round
> Then all the world would be upside down.[12]

That the Americans had defeated the English, that the child had rejected the parent, was a violation of all that seemed natural; it was the world turned upside down. For Tom Paine it was an even more dramatic rupture; it was literally a new beginning. Writing to a Frenchman about the American Revolution, the Englishman Paine talked of himself and the Americans as one. 'Our style and manner of thinking have undergone a revolution,' he wrote. 'We see with other eyes; we hear with other ears; and we think with other thoughts, than those we formerly used.'[13]

FROM STAYMAKER TO REVOLUTIONARY:
THE LIFE AND CAREER OF TOM PAINE

In 1778 Paine wrote *The Crisis*, an essay addressed to 'the People of England'. He described his feelings on arriving in America four years earlier. An unknown Englishman of thirty-seven undistinguished years, he was plunged suddenly into tumultuous Philadelphia.

I happened to come to America a few months before the breaking out of hostilities. I found the disposition of the people such, that they might have been led by a thread and governed by a reed. Their suspicion was quick and penetrating, but their attachment to Britain was obstinate, and it was at that time a kind of treason to speak against it. They disliked the ministry, but they esteemed the nation. Their idea of grievance operated without resentment, and their single object was reconciliation ... I viewed the dispute as a kind of lawsuit, in which I supposed the parties would find a way either to decide or settle it. I had no thoughts of independence or of arms. The world could not then have persuaded me that I should be either a soldier or an author ... But when the country, into which I had just set my foot, was set on fire about my ears, it was time to stir. It was time for every man to stir. Those who had been long settled had something to defend, those who had just come had something to pursue; and the call and the concern was equal and universal.[14]

Who was Tom Paine, how had he come to set foot in America, and what had he come to pursue?

He was born Tom Pain in the country town of Thetford, Norfolk, on 29 January 1737. His father, Joseph Pain, was a respected Quaker staymaker, his mother the daughter of an attorney. Tom was raised a Quaker and schooled in the village from his sixth to his thirteenth year. In 1750 he was apprenticed to his father's shop where he learned the trade of making women's corsets and inserting their steel or whalebone ribs. He ran away from home at the age of sixteen and went to sea on a merchant ship only to be brought back by his father. Three years later he left Thetford for good.

Staymaking was his trade. In 1757 he turned up in London as a journeyman staymaker and a year later in Dover. He then moved on to the small village of Sandwich on the coast where he opened a shop of his own. There he met and married, in 1759, Mary Lambert, a maid in service to the local woolen draper's wife. It was a short-lived marriage for she died the next year. Two years later Pain abandoned staymaking and started a new career as exciseman, a customs official assigned to collect the internal duties levied on beverages, tobacco and other household items. For the next few years he was assigned to Lincolnshire. In 1765 he lost his job because he had stamped goods that he had not, in fact, examined. A one-year return to staymaking in the village of Diss in Norfolk was followed by some months teaching English in London and several more as tutor and itinerant preacher. Pain was reinstated in the Excise Service in 1768 and assigned to Lewes in Sussex where he remained for the next six years.

Having settled down in Lewes at the age of thirty-one, Pain turned to politics, business and family. He became a regular at the White Hart social club where national and parish politics were the constant topics of conversation. Contemporaries later noted what a joy it was to hear young Tom Pain take on the town officers in debate after a few beers. It was a reputation that would haunt Pain all his life. In addition to politics and drink Pain devoted a good deal of the time left over from his official excise duties to a snuff, tobacco and grocery business. He had little head for business and the shop fared poorly. He also remarried in Lewes, the daughter, ten years his junior, of the former owner of his shop. In April 1774 the business failed. The marriage did no better; he and his second wife were permanently separated.

There was one important and enduring achievement in those six years in Lewes, however. Pain found his first cause and he threw himself into it with the same zeal that he would later bring to the American and French Revolutions. Excise officers throughout Britain were seeking higher salaries in the 1770s and in 1772 Pain drafted a pamphlet, *The Case of the Officers of Excise,* to make their case. He went so far as to spend a winter in London distributing copies to Members of Parliament. The cause failed, too, but Pain was in print and his appetite for social reform had been whetted. The six months in London lost him his job in the excise service, however; he was dismissed in 1774 for having left his post.

Bankrupt, separated and jobless, Pain left Lewes in 1774 and headed for London. He had not done much with his life in his thirty-seven years. He had failed in business, in marriage and in vocation. America tempted him. It offered a fresh start far from the drudgery of collecting taxes or making ladies' stays. Through connections made in the unsuccessful excise campaign Pain was introduced in London to Benjamin Franklin, then acting as agent for Pennsylvania. Franklin agreed to give Pain some letters of introduction to take to America. Franklin's note indicates how little he or any one expected from Pain. He wrote his son-in-law, a Philadelphia merchant:

The bearer Mr Thomas Pain is very well recommended to me, as an ingenious, worthy young man. He goes to Pennsylvania with a view of settling there. I request you give to him your best advice and countenance, as he is quite a stranger there. If you can put him in a way of obtaining employment as a clerk, or assistant tutor in a school, or assistant surveyor, (of all which I think him very capable) so that he may procure a subsistence at least, till he can make acquaintance and obtain a knowledge of the country, you will do well, and much oblige your affectionate father.[15]

In Philadelphia Pain tried his hand first at teaching. But he was soon persuaded to write by the printer of the *Pennsylvania Magazine*, himself a recently arrived Scotsman. Throughout 1775 Pain wrote short miscellaneous pieces for Philadelphia newspapers and magazines. One was an important and outspoken attack on slavery. In the *Pennsylvania Magazine*, which Pain edited, he wrote scientific articles as well as political ones. His interests were wide-ranging and instinctively progressive. In August 1775, for example, he published a plea for women's rights:

Even in countries where they may be esteemed the most happy [women are] constrained in their desires in the disposal of their goods; robbed of freedom and will by the laws; slaves of opinion which rules them with absolute sway and construes the slightest appearances into guilt; surrounded on all sides by judges who are at once tyrants and their seducers ... for even with changes in attitudes and laws, deeply engrained and oppressing social prejudices remain which confront women minute by minute, day by day.[16]

Pain left the *Pennsylvania Magazine* and in November 1775 began writing his anonymous essay *Common Sense*. The pamphlet appeared for sale on 10 January 1776. The author line simply read 'written by an Englishman'. Pain was angry at his publisher, who reacted to the pamphlet's immediate success by rushing out a second edition. Pain himself put out his own second edition on 14 February 1776, enlarging the pamphlet by a third. He dropped 'written by an Englishman' and told his readers to stop worrying about the author's identity and to read him instead. At the same time, Pain started adding an 'e' to his name. He was no longer an Englishman. He was a new man, a successful American; he was Tom Paine.

The plea for independence boldly urged in *Common Sense* caught the public imagination. The pamphlet 'struck a string which required but a touch to make it vibrate', a contemporary noted. 'The country was ripe for independence, and only needed somebody to tell the people so, with decision, boldness and plausibility.' Edmund Randolph of Virginia later noted that 'the public sentiment which a few weeks before [the publication of *Common Sense*] had shuddered at the tremendous obstacles, with which independence was environed, overleaped every barrier.' General Washington commented that increased hostilities, 'added to the sound doctrine and unanswerable reasoning contained in the pamphlet *Common Sense*, will not leave numbers at a loss to decide upon the propriety of a separation'. In Massachusetts a citizen noted that he believed 'no pages was ever more eagerly read, nor more generally approved. People speak of it in rapturous praise.' In Philadelphia the book made numerous converts. In sending the pamphlet to a friend in London a contemporary of Paine's noted that '*Common Sense* which I herewith send you is read to all ranks; and as many as read, so many became converted; though perhaps the hour before were most violent against the least idea of independence'.[17] George Trevelyan in his *History of the American Revolution* has summarized the impact of this pamphlet, which by February everyone knew was from the pen of Tom Paine.

It would be difficult to name any human composition which has had an effect at once so instant, so extended and so lasting ... It was pirated, parodied and imitated, and translated into the language of every country where the new republic had well-wishers. It worked nothing short of miracles and turned Tories into Whigs.

Some Tories, however, refused to budge. One such stalwart was James Chalmers, who answered Paine's

Common Sense in a pamphlet entitled *Plain Truth*. Paine's
ideas, Chalmers wrote, were 'really an insult to our understanding'. The British Constitution 'with all its imper-
fections', he wrote, 'is, and ever will be, the pride and envy
of mankind'. Without a King and aristocracy, he warned,
'our constitution would immediately degenerate into
democracy'.[18] Paine's pamphlet had more influential
opponents as well. John Adams, for example, who shared
Paine's views on independence, feared the radicalism of the
pamphlet and the effect 'so popular a pamphlet might have
among the people'. He replied to Paine in the draft of his
Thoughts on Government which he circulated among influential patriots in the spring of 1776. Adams, a much more
conservative thinker than Paine, agreed with his call for
separation, but he trembled at its popular tone and its
prescription of a simple political system for independent
America without the complex balancing and separation of
powers inherent in the older British model. Paine's ideal
sketched in *Common Sense*, Adams wrote, was 'so demo-
cratical, without any restraint or even an attempt at any
equilibrium or counter poise, that it must produce confusion and every evil work.[19]

Chalmers and John Adams notwithstanding, far fewer
criticized Paine's pamphlet than praised it. Instant fame
came to Paine when it became known that he was the
author of *Common Sense*. But he was not a man to sit idly
in his newly acquired literary and political glory. In July
1776 he enlisted in the American army. For the next seven
years, while the war with Britain dragged on, Paine
combined his military role with journalism and produced
a series of remarkable pamphlets designed to maintain
American morale as well as to make the case for America
in England and Europe. The first of these papers, later
to be published together as *The Crisis,* appeared on 23
December 1776. Addressed to all Americans as much as to

Washington and his troops huddled in the New Jersey cold, its opening lines have remained to this day the most frequently quoted of all that Paine wrote. All America must persevere, must suffer, he wrote, for all history awaited the battle's outcome.

These are the times that try men's souls: The summer soldier and the sunshine patriot will, in this crisis, shrink from the service of his country; but he that stands it now, deserves the love and thanks of man and woman. Tyranny, like hell, is not easily conquered; yet we have this consolation with us, that the harder the conflict, the more glorious the triumph. What we obtain too cheap, we esteem too lightly.

Paine played an active role in the politics of the war period, in Pennsylvania helping to shape the new state constitution and in the nation itself carrying out important foreign assignments. After the war, however, he turned his energy primarily to scientific concerns. Like many of his contemporaries in England and America – Priestley, Price, Jefferson and Franklin among others – Paine combined political liberalism with the dream of technological and scientific progress. The ease with which political arguments could, in fact, use scientific and technical principles is illustrated beautifully in *Common Sense* with its discussions of weights and forces. In terms of his career, the project to which Paine devoted most of his energy in the 1780s was the construction of an iron bridge. Efforts to develop and finance his bridge brought Paine to France and England several times in the last years of the decade. It was this quest which innocently enough brought about the third development of Paine's meteoric career. First a failure, then an American revolutionary, Paine was destined next to emerge not as a great inventor but an English revolutionary.

English radicalism had persisted from its first explosion with Wilkes in the 1760s, gathering momentum with the

American revolution in the 1770s and the growth of the County Association movement in the 1780s. The French Revolution brought to a head middle-class discontent with the archaic and unreformed constitution. A new and progressive order had come with such apparent ease to the French that English reformers assumed that change in English institutions would follow quickly and painlessly. A heady faith in progress and the dawning of a new era swept through English intellectual and radical circles. Paine himself had been in France furthering his bridge-building interests in the winter of 1789. The hero of America, Paine was toasted in the circles of Lafayette and Jefferson, then serving as American ambassador to France. From Lafayette Paine received the key to the Bastille to bring back to Washington. He was present during the early stages of the French Revolution and was pleased by what he saw.

One Englishman much less pleased than Paine was Edmund Burke, whose *Reflections on the Revolution in France* appeared in 1790 while Paine was in England ostensibly still *en route* to America.[20] Burke's was a vicious attack on the French Jacobins and their English sympathizers. They had no reverence for the past, no respect for institutions like the Church and the aristocracy, he insisted. They tore down their entire political and social edifice and built completely anew with no effort to repair the damage. Government and society, Burke wrote, were fragile and complex entities, the product of generations of slow and imperceptible growth. No reformer's plans or blueprints could substitute for the experience of the ages. Burke's message was clear. English radicals should not copy their French counterparts; the aristocratic and hierarchical English past and present must be defended from its bourgeois enemies. The intellectual spokesmen and women for that subversive enemy replied in legions to

Burke. Godwin rose to the occasion with his *Inquiry Concerning Political Justice*, Wollstonecraft with her *Vindication of the Rights of Woman;* but none would be so powerful and so popular an answer as Tom Paine's *Rights of Man* which appeared in 1791.[21]

Once again the uncomplicated, unscholarly and unsophisticated rhetoric of Paine brought him unprecedented popular success. Paine was an instant hero in England, not only to the intellectual radicals among whom he moved, such as Blake, Holcroft, Horne Tooke, Godwin and Wollstonecraft, but to hundreds of thousands of artisans and journeymen who bought *Rights of Man* for sixpence or read it reprinted by their provincial radical association. Paine's book was more than a simple defense of the French from the obloquy heaped upon them by Burke; it was also a call to the British to replace the aristocratic institutions so praised by Burke with new liberal institutions, to replace the principle of privilege and heredity with the new ideals of talent and merit. The monarchy and the aristocracy were relics of a feudal past. Republican government rested with the people and was designed to serve their interests alone. Far from the past and its institutions weighing heavy on modern man, Paine's message was that every age and every generation acted for itself, set up its own political and social order to meet its own needs. 'The vanity and presumption of governing beyond the grave,' he wrote, 'is the most ridiculous and insolent of all tyrannies. Man has no property in man; neither has any generation a property in the generations which are to follow.'[22] It is the rights of the living that he champions, not the hoary rights of privileged classes from time immemorial.

Paine was no hero to George III's Prime Minister, William Pitt the younger. Burke wrote to dissuade people from entering the radical camp, Reeves and his mob in the

Church and King Society literally burned down the insurgents' camps, while the role of Pitt and his agents in the repressive atmosphere of the early and middle 1790s was to arrest radicals, try them and throw them in jail. In 1792 charges of seditious writings were lodged against Paine and a trial scheduled. Pitt would not allow a writer, especially one so widely read, to state freely as Paine had done in the introduction to *Rights of Man*: 'If universal peace, civilization, and commerce, are ever to be the happy lot of man, it cannot be accomplished but by a revolution in the system of governments.'[23] The mood of England had shifted dramatically in the two years since Wordsworth felt such bliss to be alive in the reflected glory of the French Revolution. On the night of 22 November 1792 a patriotic mob burned Paine's effigy at Chelmsford, Essex. According to a newspaper account:

On Wednesday last, the Effigy of that Infamous Incendiary, Tom Paine, was exhibited in this town, seated in a chair, and borne on four men's shoulders; – in one hand he held the 'Rights of Man' and under the other arm he bore a pair of stays; upon his head a mock resemblance of the Cap of Liberty, and a halter round his neck.

On a banner carried before him, was written,
'Behold a Traitor!
Who, for the base purposes of Envy, Interest and Ambition,
Would have deluged this Happy Country in B L O O D!'[24]

All they had was Paine's effigy, for, sensing the justice he would receive in an England enflamed by Pitt, Burke and Reeves, Paine had fled to France two months earlier. The trial nevertheless took place in December. Paine was found guilty *in absentia* of seditious libel, and outlawed from ever returning to Britain.

Paine remained in France for the next ten years, now entering the historical stage as French revolutionary. He was chosen delegate to the National Convention by a constituency in the department of the Oise (Versailles) and threw himself into the chaotic politics of the revolution in the critical year of internecine fighting between Girondin and Jacobin. Once again Paine was no mere bystander. In October 1792 he was appointed to the Committee of Nine to frame the new French constitution. But all was not easy for Paine in the suspicious atmosphere of Paris. He became entangled in the labyrinth of revolutionary personalities and politics. He alienated Robespierre and Marat by pleading in the convention that Louis XVI's life be spared. No one was criminal enough, he argued, for the barbarity of the death penalty. In addition, he pleaded, whatever were Louis Capet's manifest faults he had after all 'aided my much-loved America to break its chains'. The English-speaking Paine became further suspect when war broke out in 1793 between France and England. In October his allies the Girondins were tried and condemned. In December foreigners in the Convention were denounced. Paine was arrested and imprisoned.

For the ten months of his imprisonment Paine busied himself working on the first part of *The Age of Reason*, a penetrating attack on theistic Christianity and defense of a natural deistic religion free from supernatural trappings. In it he examined the Bible and regaled his readers with its contradictions, its false chronology and its tales of barbarism, slaughter and inhumanity. This was not, he argued, the work of the God who presided over the natural universe. In an age of reason, he insisted, men and women would replace such superstition with science and nature. In place of a mysterious and brutal God, they would have God the first cause, the Supreme Being. While he wrote on religion, Paine also worked on his release from prison through the good offices of the American minister, James Monroe. After some confusion about his status as American or British, Paine was released in the fall of 1794.

The Jacobins had fallen in the meantime and Robespierre himself had been guillotined. Paine was re-elected to the Assembly in December 1794 and sat through the following year, but he had contracted a malignant fever in prison and for the most part could only summon energy enough to write. His last years in Paris, therefore, were less political than polemical. He produced a second and third part of *The Age of Reason,* a long political essay, *Dissertations on the First Principles of Government,* and an important piece of social and economic criticism, *Agrarian Justice* (1797).

In 1802 Paine returned to America for the final and most tragic chapter in his career. The America he found was very different from the Philadelphia he had known in 1774 or even in 1783. The social ferment of those years had been stilled by a federal constitution and a federalist ideology which threw the balance of political and social power into the hands of the powerful and well-to-do. *Common Sense* was a thing of the distant past. Paine was no longer the celebrated author of the pamphlet so influential in its day. He was now the notorious author of the godless *Age of Reason* with its assault on Christianity. Jefferson was man enough to renew his old ties with Paine, but by most Americans the great patriot found himself forgotten or ignored.

The aging Paine, with no family and few close friends, became cantankerous and argumentative, turning more and more to the solace of drink. His last years were spent in New York City, in what is now Greenwich Village, or on his farm in New Rochelle outside the city. He died on 8 June 1809. Few people saw the coffin from the city to the farm in New Rochelle. At the burial site there were even fewer present, merely a handful of New Rochelle neighbors and friends. There were no dignitaries, no eulogies, no official notices of his death. The staymaker from Thetford who had shaped the world as few have ever done, who had known and been known by many great men of America, France and England, was laid to rest in a quiet pasture with no ceremony, no fanfare, no appreciation. The irony of such a funeral for such a man was too much for Madame de Bonneville, who had acted for several years as Paine's housekeeper, and who was one of the few present. She later wrote:

This interment was a scene to affect and to wound any sensible heart. Contemplating who it was, what man it was, that we were committing to an obscure grave on an open and disregarded bit of land, I could not help feeling most acutely. Before the earth was thrown down upon the coffin, I, placing myself at the east end of the grave, said to my son Benjamin, 'stand you there, at the other end, as a witness for grateful America'. Looking round me, and beholding the small group of spectators, I exclaimed, as the earth was tumbled into the grave, 'Oh! Mr Paine! My son stands here as testimony of the gratitude of America, and I, for France!' This was the funeral ceremony of this great politician and philosopher![25]

The irony of eclipse had not yet run its course. Ten years after his unnoticed interment, William Cobbett, an enthusiastic convert to Paine's radicalism, decided on a whim to dig up Paine's bones and return them to England, intending to erect over this new resting-place some memorial to Paine's achievement. Paine's body reached Liverpool, and it may have reached London. No one knows for sure, however, for the final indignity to Tom Paine was that Cobbett lost the bones. Such was the gratitude of America and England.

THE ARGUMENT OF *Common Sense*

The United States of America may in part owe its birth to

Common Sense, but with the exception of a brief line in the introduction, neither America nor independence is mentioned until well into the pamphlet. Why should it be otherwise? Paine had been in the colonies for only fourteen months when he published *Common Sense.* He was English, after all, and it is this which breathes through every page of his remarkable work. He brings to the burning issues of Philadelphia in 1776 the theoretical mind and raging anger of English radicalism.

The pamphlet begins with an exposition of general liberal theory, and gathers momentum with an attack on the English constitution in particular and on aristocratic institutions in general. Only then does it make sense to talk of the messianic mission of America, when it can be seen in its broadest theoretical context. An independent America and a chastened England represent the triumph of radical Republican principles and as close an approximation to the theoretical ideal sketched at the beginning of the pamphlet as is humanly possible.

The intellectual roots of Paine's first section are the late-seventeenth-century liberal ideals of John Locke and the radical critique of English society found in the writings of English dissenting ministers like Priestley, Price and Burch in the late eighteenth century. The principal assumption is, as Paine puts it, that men originally lived as isolated, free and solitary individuals in a 'state of natural liberty'. A thousand reasons draw men together; in society they provide each other with essential mutual assistance. But society and government are entirely different: 'The one encourages intercourse, the other creates distinctions.' How then does government come about; what is 'the design and end of government'? Men voluntarily set up government, according to Paine, because it 'will unavoidably happen' that these free and autonomous individuals have divergent interests which endanger one another's

natural rights to life, liberty or property. Like James
Madison, Paine insists that it is because men are not angels
that they submit themselves to government. Government,
then, is a product of human wickedness and its sole end is
to ensure 'freedom and security'. It should do no more
than this minimal chore, protect natural rights. It has no
positive function, as classical and Christian theorists had
argued, no mandate to promote virtue, the good life or
the true faith. It is a necessary evil and should be involved
in nothing more than what it is unfortunately required to
do.

Government's role, then, should be strictly limited.
It should be simple and cheap. 'Securing freedom and
property to all men, and, above all things, the free exercise
of religion', he writes, requires neither great expense nor
complicated bureaucratic apparatus. That liberal Republican government was simple was a persistent theme in
eighteenth-century literature. Monarchic and aristocratic
government was pictured as interfering government, an
overblown taxing machine that intruded too much into the
private world of free individuals, preventing the realiza-
tion of rights and achievements.

Paine's ideal was shared, for example, by Adam Smith
who in that same year (1776) published *The Wealth of
Nations* in which he drew the economic conclusion implicit
in their common notions. Government, Smith wrote, was
to refrain from interfering 'with that natural liberty, which
it is the proper business of law not to infringe'.[26] Smith's
and Paine's is the basic liberal vision. The social order and
the economy are spontaneous and self-regulating mechan-
isms, peopled by rational, self-seeking individuals. It is a
harmonious society, as Smith put it, where without

any intervention of law, the private interests and passions of
men naturally lead them to divide and distribute the stock of

every society among all the different employments carried on in it, as nearly as possible in proportion which is most agreeable to the interest of the whole society.[27]

Government, according to both Paine and Smith, merely presides passively over this self-regulating economy and spontaneously harmonious polity. At most, it is the umpire that enforces the rules, the most important of which is the 'secure enjoyment of the fruits of his own labour'. It is, Smith wrote, 'only under the shelter of the civil magistrate that the owner of that valuable property which is acquired by the labour of many years or perhaps of many successive generations can sleep a single night in security'.[28] Both Paine and Smith had read their Locke.

But Paine brought more than Lockean liberalism to *Common Sense*, he also brought the rage of English radicalism. British government is attacked in this pamphlet with all the savagery that one finds in the London defenders of John Wilkes and all the fiery passion that one finds among the Unitarian and Calvinist opponents of the Test and Corporation Acts which excluded dissenting Protestants from government and municipal positions and from Oxford and Cambridge. Nowhere in the pamphlet does Paine itemize the grievances of the colonies. It is simply taken for granted that their treatment by the English government violates universal reason and natural rights. It is an 'exceedingly complex' and exceptionally corrupt engine of oppression that hangs as a weight upon the energetic Americans as it does upon the virtuous English.

One particular group of Englishmen that sensed themselves oppressed was the talented middle class. And it is their grievances that Paine and his radical colleagues in England articulated in the assault on the monarchic and aristocratic principle. Traditional society assumed certain natural distinctions which, as Paine noted, exalted certain ranks above others. Society was conceived of as divided into natural gradations of status and power descending from the monarchy through the aristocratic ranks down to the commoners. Where one fit into this hierarchical order was determined by birth. In turn prestige, power and privilege were also accorded individuals by dint of rank and distinction. Against this aristocratic ideal the bourgeoisie, whose articulate ranks were being swelled by the successful entrepreneurs of the industrial revolution, offered a new ideal: that of careers and rewards open to the talented. Armed with a vision of 'mankind being originally equal in the order of creation', as Paine put it, the middle class attacked the dominance of idle monarchs and useless aristocrats in society and politics and demanded in turn an end to all elements of traditional privileges which froze individuals into permanent inequality. What mattered was not lineage but talent and merit. Here, too, the British were sinful violators of God's natural equality as they set up luxurious and foolish men of no skills to rule over the industrious, hardworking and unenfranchised middle class.

One is reminded that dissenting Protestantism was a critical component of the ideology of the talented bourgeoisie by the importance Paine gives to scriptural, primarily Old Testament, injunctions against monarchy and aristocratic distinctions in general. It provides a link with the leveling radicalism of the seventeenth-century civil-war sects, many of whose descendants had emigrated to the more egalitarian shores of America and to the many religious entrepreneurs of the late eighteenth century who threatened to leave for America if the religious exclusiveness of the Anglican establishment were not modified. The Quaker Tom Paine knew his audience well and knew that Biblical arguments against the British and even an occasional anti-Catholic note would move them. He also knew that hard-working, self-reliant Americans had no love for the hereditary principle by which a man has 'a right to set up his own family in perpetual preference to all others forever'. Not only can few titles bear close inspection without being revealed as founded in plunder and conquest, but more critically the whole system of frozen ranks and ascribed status was 'unwise', 'unjust' and 'unnatural'.

After his assault on aristocratic and hereditary principles Paine turns finally to 'the present state of American affairs'. His interest is that of an English radical convinced that America's destiny transcends the mere livelihood of the people of the thirteen colonies in January 1776. America stands as the living repudiation of the old aristocratic and monarchic order. Her independence strikes the first blow in the battle to overthrow the *ancien régime*, it will help undermine the dominant position of the crown in public life, it will subvert the corrupt system of George III and the burdensome taxes of his ministers. But Paine's vision is more grandiose still. America's independence had meta-historical significance – it will usher in a new era in world history.

Paine's rhetoric in *Common Sense* reminds his readers, indeed flatters his fundamentalist readers, that the independence of the thirteen colonies is an event of momentous importance, not unlike the dramatic events told of in the scriptures. Like the Hebrews, the Americans are invested with a messianic mission. 'The cause of America is in a great measure the cause of all mankind,' Paine points out in the introduction. The scriptural tone is repeated when later in the pamphlet he notes that 'posterity are virtually involved in the contest, and will be more or less affected, even to the end of time, by the proceedings now'. American independence is a flood which will wipe clean the slate of history. America has it in her power, Paine writes, 'to begin the world over again. A situation, similar to the present, hath not happened since the days of Noah until now. The birthday of a new world is at hand.' Paine's flight of fancy, his sense of the American mission, reads on occasion like pure poetry. There is no more stirring passage in *Common Sense* than the evocation of America's destiny which to this day expresses an aspect of American idealism:

O ye that love mankind! Ye that dare oppose, not only the tyranny, but the tyrant, stand forth! Every spot of the old world is over-run with oppression. Freedom hath been hunted round the globe. Asia, and Africa, have long expelled her. – Europe regards her like a stranger, and England hath given her warning to depart. O! receive the fugitive, and prepare in time an asylum for mankind.*

Paine is seldom concerned with the petty details of colonial grievances. He had had little time to learn them in his fourteen months in Philadelphia. No recital here of confiscations or unjust taxation policy, massacres or reneged charter rights. What is important, he tells his readers, is that America dissociate itself from England. It is not a matter of grievances but of a world-historical mission. America's destiny is to usher in a new age, in which there would no longer be wrathful master stay-makers chafing under stifling and oppressive aristocratic institutions.

Paine's pamphlet was no mere recital of ministerial blunders, no learned disquisition on constitutional or imperial theory. His readers were summoned to greatness, recruited for a crusade against the old world and the values from which so many Americans had fled. America was crucial to Paine's vision of the new world order, and, not surprisingly, the passion and fervor of the pamphlet is to be found in the first part of the work and in the passages

* See below, p. 102.

describing America's mission. In contrast, when Paine begins to argue in detail the case for separation and independence, his tone changes and he starts to talk the language of common sense.

The practical case for independence is an impressive one. America has no need for commercial ties with England, Paine insists. There are enough markets for American corn 'while eating is the custom of Europe'. Reconciliation with England will, on the other hand, involve America in all the quarrels and wars of Europe. An independent and thus peaceful America provides security for property. Under the English property is precarious. The mother country only cares for the good of America if it serves her own interests. When these interests conflict with colonial interests 'her own interest leads her to suppress the growth of ours'. Prospective emigrants will think twice about coming to America if there is to be no security for property, if it is always to be at the mercy of England's interest. 'The property of no man is secure in the present unbraced system of things.' Nor can English rule ever really be effective, according to Paine. The thousands of miles, the months of delay make it impossible for England properly to manage the colonies.

This is the commonsense case for independence. Occasionally, however, Paine lifts his pen from the commercial ledger and points to reasons for separation that transcend the mundane. It is, for example, historically decreed, 'an event which sooner or later must arrive'. Elsewhere he notes that America's continued dependence on England is 'repugnant to reason, to the universal order of things'. This is more than the effrontery to nature of an island ruling a continent; it is also a violation of the rights of humanity derived from God and nature.

Should some of his readers be reluctant to separate from England for lack of any alternative system of government, Paine offers his own constitutional plan. A popular convention consisting of provincial delegates will produce a charter guaranteeing the freedom and free exercise of religion for all. The new government will be cheap, operating 'with the least national expence'. Property will be secure. There will be no kings or ministerial taxes to interfere with property rights, nor will 'the desperate and the discontented' sweep away the liberties of the continent. In America 'the law is King'.

The argument turns next to America's ability to exist free of English influence and resist English rule. Paine is convinced that America can raise a fleet and equip an impressive army. There is some confusion on his part about national debts: on one page he delights that America is free of this burden, on another he boasts that to fight a long war America will incur a huge debt and that 'no nation ought to be without a debt'. It is in the realm of common sense that the pamphlet bogs down. Paine moves few readers with his excursions into finance and commerce.

Only in its final pages when Paine again leaves common sense for rhetorical exhortation does the pamphlet come to life once more. Paine's attack on the passivity and non-resistance of his fellow Quakers is a charge to all Americans not to be 'the quiet and inoffensive subject of any and every government which is set over him'. He proclaims that 'setting up and putting down Kings and governments' is the natural right of citizens. There are no given ranks of authority and subordination and no one need fear appearing 'to be busy bodies above our station'. This is the angry Paine that Americans read when they devoured his pamphlet. It was not Tom Paine's common sense but his rage that turned hundreds of thousands of Americans to thoughts of independence in the winter of 1776.

In one of his novels, Robert Bage, a late-eighteenth-century English radical novelist, indicated the passing of the old order by describing a change in the reading habits of his hero. 'In my youth I also read tragedies, epic poems, romances, and divinity. Now I read *Common Sense*.'[29] Tom Paine's pamphlet became the symbol of the age, the passing of the traditional aristocratic order and its replacement by liberal bourgeois values. But the author of *Common Sense* was no ordinary radical. His was perhaps the most devastating assault on the old order that could be found in the bourgeois camp. Burke wrote of Paine that he sought to destroy 'in six or seven days' the feudal and chivalric world which 'all the boasted wisdom of our ancestors has labored to bring to perfection for six or seven centuries'.[30] Part of Paine's achievement was indeed to mock the past so venerated by Burke. For Paine it was 'the Quixotic age of chivalric nonsense'.[31] He ridiculed the ancient principles of British society, beginning in *Common Sense* with the useless and unproductive monarchy.

In England a king hath little more to do than to make war and give away places; which in plain terms, is to impoverish the nation and set it together by the ears. A pretty business indeed for a man to be allowed eight hundred thousand sterling a year for, and worshipped into the bargain! Of more worth is one honest man to society and in the sight of God, than all the crowned ruffians that ever lived.*

Is there anything more absurd than the hereditary principle, Paine asked in *Rights of Man*, 'as absurd as an hereditary mathematician, or an hereditary wise man, and as ridiculous as an hereditary poet-laureate?'[32] What mattered was not a man's pedigree but his productivity.

* See below, p. 83.

This was the message of Adam Smith, and Paine berates his arch-opponent Burke in *Rights of Man* for his false reasoning which he would have recanted 'had Mr Burke possessed talents similar to the author of *On the Wealth of Nations*'.[33] Government required 'talents and abilities', yet its offices were filled by a nobility which, according to Paine, really meant 'no-ability'.[34] The aristocracy were unproductive idlers, parasites who lived off the work of the industrious classes. No one would miss them in a reconstructed rational society.

Why then does Mr Burke talk of his house of peers, as the pillar of the landed interest? Were that pillar to sink into the earth, the same landed property would continue, and the same ploughing, sowing, and reaping would go on. The aristocracy are not the farmers who work the land, and raise the produce, but are the mere consumers of the rent; and when compared with the active world are the drones . . . who neither collect the honey nor form the hive, but exist only for lazy enjoyment.[35]

This fierce egalitarianism endeared Paine to the working man. It was applauded in the 1790s by the artisans of the London Corresponding Society and by factory workers who in droves purchased his *Rights of Man* for sixpence. But reading Paine around the 'liberty tree' does not in itself make him a working-class ideologue. His merciless indictment and repudiation of an aristocratic polity and society did serve the interests of the workers and touched their souls. But at this juncture of history their cause lay with the bourgeois destruction of aristocratic England, and it was that cause that consumed Paine in his *Rights of Man* as it did throughout his entire career. There is really little contradiction between Paine's radical egalitarian views and his defense of property and business enterprise. Paine, even in America, was an English radical, nurtured in an aristocratic society. Bourgeois ideals were in his mind inextricably linked with an egalitarian vision of

society. The stratified society of privilege and rank per-
petuated by the hereditary principle would be leveled in
a bourgeois world where political and social place would be
determined by talent, merit and hard work. To be a fierce
egalitarian, to be acutely sensitive to injustice, was by no
means incompatible in this era with being bourgeois;
indeed, for some time in England the two would be by no
means contradictory. Only in America and other societies
which lacked an oppressive and hierarchical past was there
a problem in being both a bourgeois ideologue and an
egalitarian. But even here the two were by no means always mutually exclusive, for liberal egalitarianism does not
insist on equality of conditions, but only equality of opportunity.

It detracts in no way from the progressive and humani-
tarian quality of Paine's scathing indictment of the old
order to note its bourgeois dimensions. These, indeed,
were the terms such an attack necessarily took at this
juncture of history. He was no less a radical for writing in
his essay defending the Bank of Pennsylvania that the
foundation of the Republic is 'the security to the rich and
the consolation to the poor . . . that what each man has is
his own, that no despotic government can take it from
him,'[36] nor for his fears that the majority of unproper-
tied, 'the despotism of numbers', might invade the property and contractual rights of the few. Nevertheless, it
should not be forgotten that Paine's most radical social
proposals, his suggestion, for example, in *Agrarian
Justice* that fifteen pounds be paid to every person at the
age of twenty-one and that ten pounds per year be paid
to all over fifty years of age, were much more anti-aristo-
cratic in intent than anti-bourgeois. He wrote in *Agrarian
Justice* of the original commonality of land, but so had
Locke. What really infuriated Paine was that a yeoman
republic of independent landed owners did not exist and

that instead there evolved an aristocratic society based fundamentally on huge territorial holdings. His remedy for the injustice involved in this usurpation of the people's 'natural inheritance' was certainly advanced for his day, and would later become the basis for important radical and socialist demands. But his proposed 10 per cent inheritance tax and his direct grants of money were offered primarily as salvos against the pernicious aristocractic order. Their ultimate purpose was to underwrite a redistribution of wealth and power which would be based on equality of opportunity and which would thus enable talented and industrious men of real ability to replace those of 'no-ability'. His equally celebrated proposals in Part II of *Rights of Man* for the redistribution to the poor of money saved by dismantling the war machinery and eliminating excess public offices would, he insisted over and over again, have an objective even more useful. It would relieve the overburdened middle class of its taxes and especially of its most onerous burden, the poor rates.

Paine was one of the purest ideological spokesmen for the bourgeoisie, exhorting them to take over the state. The demand was expressed in the language of economic determinism; the political order, he insisted, must mirror the realities of economic power.

Whether the forms and maxims of Governments which are still in practice, were adapted to the condition of the world at the period they were established, is not in this case the question. The older they are, the less correspondence can they have with the present state of things. Time, and change of circumstances and opinions, have the same progressive effect in rendering modes of Government obsolete, as they have upon customs and manners. Agriculture, commerce, manufactures, and the tranquil arts, by which the prosperity of Nations is best promoted, require a different system of Government, and a different species of knowledge to direct its operations, than what might have been required in the former condition of the world.[37]

Once in control of the state the bourgeoisie would proceed to simplify and streamline its institutional apparatus. The size of government would be reduced dramatically and it would be made inexpensive.

Government is nothing more than a national association; and the object of this association is the good of all, as well individually as collectively. Every man wishes to pursue his occupation, and to enjoy the fruits of his labours, and the produce of his property in peace and safety, and with it the least possible expense. When these things are accomplished, all the objects for which government ought to be established are answered.[38]

Liberal society, according to Paine, has no unity, no consensus. Cooperation and fellowship are not characteristic of it. Like Smith and Madison, and like liberal apologists to this day, Paine gloried in the conflict and competition that was at the heart of liberalism. It was not a twentieth-century pluralist defending liberal democracy who wrote:

A nation is composed of distinct, unconnected individuals, following various trades, employments and pursuits; continually meeting, crossing, uniting, opposing and separating from each other, as accident, interest, and circumstance shall direct.[39]

Government was not a positive agent laying the foundation for a just or good society, let alone a welfare state. Its only role was to provide a stable and secure setting for the operations of a commercial society.

What would happen, Paine asked in *Common Sense*, if England continued her rule in America? Chaos and uncertainty, disastrously unsettling to the economic foundations of society, would inevitably follow.

Emigrants of property will not choose to come to a country whose form of government hangs but by a thread, and who is every day tottering on the brink of commotion and disturbance; and numbers of the present inhabitants would lay hold of the interval, to dispose of their effects, and quit the continent.*

Along with its other defects government in the old order not only failed to provide the security essential for man to enjoy the fruits of his labor; it was also itself the major factor upsetting his peace and safety and stealing from him his very produce and property through taxation.

When we survey the wretched condition of man under the monarchical and hereditary systems of Government, dragged from his home by one power, or driven by another, and impoverished by taxes more than by enemies, it becomes evident that those systems are bad, and that a general revolution in the principle and construction of Governments is necessary.[40]

Tyranny, for Paine, was taxation. He constantly returned to this theme. In his *Prospects on the Rubicon* (1787) he described himself defending 'the cause of the poor, of the manufacturers, of the tradesmen, of the farmer, and of all those on whom the real burden of taxes fall . . .'[41] Monarchy, aristocracy and taxes were all of a piece in Paine's mind. In his *Anti-Monarchical Essay* (1792) he insisted that 'in a word, whoever demands a king, demands an aristocracy, and thirty millions of taxes'. Royalty, he was sure, 'has been invented only to obtain from men excessive taxes . . .'[42] The turmoil of the revolutionary age was, in fact, produced by angry taxpayers who had had enough. He wrote in 1792:

There are two distinct classes of men in the Nation [England], those who pay taxes and those who receive and live upon the taxes . . . When taxation is carried to excess, it cannot fail to disunite those two, and something of this is now beginning to appear.[43]

*See below, p. 96.

Revolution was necessary to bring about governments 'less expensive, and more productive of general happiness', and the reign of 'peace, civilization, and commerce'.[44] The customary and traditional attachment to older forms would evaporate before 'the test of reason'. 'Prejudices are nothing,' Paine wrote; 'reason, like time, will make its own way, and prejudice will fall in a combat with interest.'[45] 'Reason' here meant the bourgeois reason of calculated and material utility. Progress had been made in England, Paine suggested, by enterprising and calculating individuals in spite of and in disregard of government:

It is from the enterprise and industry of the individuals, and their numerous associations, in which, tritely speaking, government is neither pillow nor bolster, that these improvements have proceeded. No man thought about the government, or who was *in,* or who was *out,* when he was planning or executing those things; and all he had to hope, with respect to government, was, *that it would let him alone.*[46]

Enterprising individuals left alone by government would not produce a completely egalitarian social structure, however. Good bourgeois liberal that he was, Paine saw the post-revolutionary order free of the aristocracy but still characterized by economic differentiation. 'That property will ever be unequal is certain,' he wrote in 1795. This was not unjust, but simply a result of 'industry, superiority of talents, dexterity of management, extreme frugality, and fortunate opportunities'.[47]

The revolutionary Paine had seen the future in America. It was the spark that set off the flame of bourgeois revolution in Europe. It was a new Athens, 'the admiration and model for the present'. America ushered in a new era in human history, the 'birth day of a new world', a world dominated by republican principles and bourgeois ideals. This millenarian mission could even be rendered in mechanical terms. Paine, the engineer, likened America's destiny to Archimedes' famous quest. "Had we," said he, "a place to stand upon, we might raise the world." The revolution of America presented in politics what was only theory in mechanics.'[48]

American government was inexpensive. The civil list for the support of one man, the King of England, Paine noted, 'is eight times greater than the whole expense of the federal government in America'. It was also simple and understandable. The Americans put into practice Paine's maxim that the 'sum of necessary government is much less than is generally thought'.[49] There was no room in the limited scope of American government for the craft and obfuscation of courts. Everyone understood the operation of government there; nothing was hidden in recesses of complexity and arcane knowledge. 'There is no place for mystery; nowhere for it to begin.' In *Common Sense* Paine praised the simplicity of American government as 'less liable . . . to be disordered'. By contrast, 'the constitution of England is so exceedingly complex' that its ills endure for years while the source of the fault is hunted down. The advantages of government in America are all interrelated. It is only by getting men to believe 'that government is some wonderful mysterious thing, that excessive revenues are obtained,' Paine wrote.[50]

Finally, government in America, to which the world would soon turn, was representative government, firmly rooted in the consent of the governed. Here, too, Paine the bourgeois radical is evident. Describing the profound revolution that is popular government he reads like the often-parodied bourgeois liberal describing government as a joint stock company. Not only was his image of American government that of a business enterprise, but his description of consent and representation was rendered in the cost-accounting language of capitalism. He wrote of free America:

Every man is a proprietor in government, and considers it a necessary part of his business to understand. It concerns his interest, because it effects his property. He examines the cost, and compares it with the advantages; and above all, he does not adopt the slavish custom of following what in other governments are called LEADERS.[51]

Government was founded in America, Paine wrote, on 'a moral theory', on the 'indefeasible, hereditary Rights of Man'.[52] And it was this spirit, Paine suggested, which was sweeping from West to East. Government based on this moral theory had dramatic social and economic implications. In *Rights of Man* Paine's message was that these, too, would soon cross the Atlantic.

There [America], the poor are not oppressed, the rich are not privileged. Industry is not mortified by the splendid extravagance of a court rioting at its expense. There taxes are few, because their government is just.[53]

The English were getting the revolutionary message, according to Paine. In 1792 he wrote that calls for change were coming fast to England. It was 'far greater than could have been believed and it was daily and hourly increasing . . . The enormous expense of government has provoked men to think.'[54] What drove men to revolution seems to have been neither moral revulsion, nor physical compulsion, but simply a taxing and overblown government.

To emphasize the bourgeois Paine is not to discount the Paine who later would become a hero for the Chartists and early trade unionists. It is simply to insist that his radicalism be seen as still within the bourgeois fold, a line of interpretation receiving little stress in recent discussions of his politics. There is no doubt that while other bourgeois radicals may have just as bitterly assailed the higher ranks of privilege few could match Paine in his sympathy for the lower ranks of the poor and destitute. This was by no means the major emphasis in his writings. Nevertheless, it informed the brilliant series of policy reforms he advocated which anticipated so much of twentieth-century social welfare legislation.

There is no doubt, then, that Paine pushed bourgeois radicalism to its outermost limits and that in doing this he represented for the conservatives of his era a dangerous influence. John Adams, for example, America's second president, beautifully personified this fear of Paine. A leader of colonial protest against England, an advocate of independence, Adams had never lost his basic conservative ideals. The radical and egalitarian vision of Paine offended Adams's sense of the given and proper ranks that necessarily structure the social order. Adams sensed the evil even in *Common Sense*, calling it 'a poor, ignorant, malicious, short sighted, crapulous mass'. In a letter of 1805 Adams wrote:

I know not whether any man in the world has had more influence on its inhabitants or affairs for the last thirty years than Tom Paine. There can be no severer satyr on the age. For such a mongrel between pig and puppy, begotten by a wild boar on a bitch wolf, never before in any age of the world was suffered by the poltronnery of mankind, to run through such a career of mischief. Call it then the Age of Paine.[55]

PAINE AND THE AMERICAN BICENTENNIAL

Notorious in his own time, Paine fared little better at the hands of later generations. He proved too radical for the bourgeoisie of the Anglo-American world as that class triumphed and took the reigns of power. The egalitarianism of his message and its assault on privilege and rank seemed subversive when the bourgeoisie itself assumed the posture of a privileged class against challenges from the left. Another element was the reaction against free thinking that characterized post-Enlightenment England and America; Tom Paine was doubly cursed, for Paine was also the anti-Christ of the *Age of Reason*. He did live on in the nineteenth-century British working-class movement, to be sure, as a theorist of equality and critic of privilege. But even here his reputation sat uneasily with the chapel-based proletariat.

Slowly Paine has begun to receive his due in this century. His books have been republished and his reputation rehabilitated. After 120 years of biographies emphasizing subversion, atheism and drunkenness, one finds biographies detailing his amazingly productive life, and monographs dealing with the intricacies of his thought.

Nowadays, Tom Paine societies abound in America and England. A statue of Paine was erected in Thetford in 1964, and a pub, 'The Rights of Man', built on the Thetford motorway in 1968, complete with a 'Tom Paine Lounge', its walls decorated with posters of early Paine editions. Paine might have liked this tribute. In America his face was put on a postage stamp in 1968 (he might have liked the symbolism of that, too) and his farmhouse in New Rochelle has been restored for the edification of tourists and schoolchildren. But it is only as America celebrates its bicentennial that it makes amends for the cruel torment it inflicted on Paine in his last years and at his death. Only now as the books and articles praising Paine's life and writings flow from the presses is there truly 'a witness for grateful America'. But more important than the ceremony, fanfare and appreciation Paine justly deserves is the recommitment to his fundamental conviction, the assault on unjustified privilege. The appeal of *Common Sense* in 1776 was to America; in 1976 it is to her and to all peoples.

'Freedom hath been hunted round the globe ... O! receive the fugitive, and prepare in time an asylum for mankind.'

NOTES TO EDITOR'S INTRODUCTION

1. Quoted in Bernard Bailyn's 'Common Sense', *Fundamental Testaments of the American Revolution* (Washington, D.C., 1973), p. 7.

2. 'Examination of Benjamin Franklin in the House of Commons', 13 February 1766, in J. P. Greene, ed., *Colonies to Nation: 1763–1789* (New York, 1967), p. 73.

3. The following few paragraphs are based on the excellent analysis by Professor Greene in his 'An Uneasy Connection: An Analysis of the Preconditions of the American Revolution', in *Essays on the American Revolution*, S. G. Kurtz and J. H. Hutson, eds. (New York, 1973).

4. 'On the Right to Tax America', in M. Platz, ed. *Anthology of Public Speeches* (New York, 1940), p. 407.

5. 'Letters from a Farmer in Pennsylvania to the Inhabitants of the British Colonies' in *Tracts of the American Revolution,* edited by M. Jensen (Indianapolis, 1967), p. 127ff.

6. Quoted in H. J. Carman, H. C. Syrett and B. W. Wishy, *A History of the American People* (New York, 1961), I, p. 175.

7. ibid., I, p. 185.

8. ibid., I, p. 186.

9. 'Speech on Moving His Resolutions for Conciliation with America', in *The Works of the Right Honourable Edmund Burke* (London, 1883), I, p. 456ff.

10. For a penetrating discussion of this English connection, see Pauline Maier's *From Resistance to Revolution* (New York, 1974). These passages are from pp. 257–8.

11. ibid., p. 270.

12. An account of this incident is found in Samuel Elliot Morrison's *Oxford History of the American People* (New York, 1965), p. 265.

13. Tom Paine, 'Letter to Abbé Raynal on the Affairs of North America', in *The Writings of Thomas Paine*, ed. M. D. Conway and C. Putnam (New York, 1906), II, p. 105.

14. Number VII, 'To the People of England', in *The Crisis* (Philadelphia, 21 November 1778).

15. Cited in David Freeman Hawke's *Paine* (New York, 1974), p. 20.

16. 'An Occasional Letter to the Female Sex' (1775), in *The Writings of Thomas Paine*, op. cit., II, p. 60.

17. Hawke, *Paine*, op. cit., pp. 47–8.

18. Cited in Bernard Bailyn, *The Ideological Origins of the American Revolution* (Cambridge, Mass., 1967), p. 287.

19. ibid., p. 289.

20. See Pelican Classics edition, ed. Conor Cruise O'Brien (Harmondsworth, 1968).

21. For Godwin, see Pelican Classics edition, ed. Isaac Kramnick (Harmondsworth, 1976); for Wollstonecraft, see Pelican Classics edition, ed. Miriam Brody Kramnick (Harmondsworth, 1975); for *Rights of Man*, see Pelican Classics edition, ed. Henry Collins (Harmondsworth, 1969).

22. *Rights of Man*, op. cit., pp. 63–4.

23. ibid., p. 183.

24. Cited in Audrey Williamson, *Thomas Paine* (New York, 1973), pp. 160–61.

25. ibid., p. 275.

26. Adam Smith, *The Wealth of Nations* (New York, 1937), p. 340.

27. ibid., pp. 594–5.

28. ibid., pp. 508, 610.

29. Robert Bage, *The Fair Syrian* (London, 1787), I, p. 43.

30. Edmund Burke, 'Letters on a Regicide Peace', in *Works*, op. cit., V, p. 395.

31. *Rights of Man*, op. cit., p. 72.

32. ibid., p. 105.

33. ibid., p. 97.

34. ibid., p. 128.

35. ibid., p. 249.

36. Tom Paine, 'Dissertations on Government, the Affairs of the Bank and Paper Money' (Philadelphia, 1786), in *The Writings of Thomas Paine*, op. cit., III, p. 138.

37. *Rights of Man*, op. cit., p. 168.

38. ibid., p. 220.

39. 'Dissertations on Government . . .', in *The Writings of Thomas Paine*, op. cit., III, p. 137.

40. *Rights of Man*, op. cit., p. 165.

41. (Paris, 1787), in *The Writings of Tom Paine*, op. cit., III, p. 204.

42. (Paris, 1792), ibid., III, p. 107.

43. 'Letter Addressed to the Addressers on the Late Proclama-

tion', (London, 1792), in *The Writings of Thomas Paine*, op. cit., III, p. 55.

44. *Rights of Man,* op. cit., p. 183.

45. ibid., pp. 179, 183.

46. ibid., p. 219 fn.

47. 'Dissertation on First Principles of Government' (Paris, 1795), in *The Writings of Thomas Paine*, op. cit., III, p. 268.

48. *Rights of Man,* op. cit., p. 181.

49. 'Thomas Paine's Answer to Four Questions on the Legislative and Executive Powers' (Paris, 1791), in *The Writings of Thomas Paine*, op. cit., III, p. 245.

50. *Rights of Man,* op. cit., p. 206.

51. ibid; the capitalization is Paine's.

52. ibid., pp. 183–4.

53. ibid., p. 189.

54. 'Letter Addressed to the Addressers on the Late Proclamation', in *The Writings of Thomas Paine*, op. cit., III. p. 81.

55. Cited in *Paine,* op. cit., p. 7.

A NOTE ON THE TEXT

The text used here is the second edition of *Common Sense* published on 14 February 1776 by William and Thomas Bradford of Philadelphia, Pennsylvania. The first edition, substantially shorter, was published on 10 January 1776 by the Philadelphia firm of Robert Bell. Paine had intended that his share of the profits from the January printing be used for purchasing mittens for the colonial forces fighting in Quebec. He was furious to learn that Bell had no profits to divide and assumed he had been cheated. Because of this, Paine took his second enlarged edition, with its appendix and reply to the Quaker meeting of 20 January, to a new publisher. It is this 'enlarged edition', one third longer than the first, which we reproduce here.

SUGGESTIONS FOR FURTHER READINGS

A. PAINE'S WRITINGS:

The Rights of Man, ed. Henry Collins (Penguin Books, Harmondsworth, 1969).
The Age of Reason (New York, 1948).
The Writings of Thomas Paine, ed. M. D. Conway and C. Putnam (New York, 1906).

B. BIOGRAPHIES OF PAINE:

Aldridge, A. O., *Man of Reason: The Life of Thomas Paine* (New York, 1959).
Conway, M. D., *The Life of Thomas Paine* (New York and London, 1892), 2 vols.
Hawke, David Freeman, *Paine* (New York, 1974).
Williamson, Audrey, *Thomas Paine: His Life, Work and Times* (New York, 1973).

C. CONTEXTUAL STUDIES RELEVANT TO PAINE:

Bailyn, Bernard, *The Ideological Origins of the American Revolution* (Cambridge, Mass., 1967).
Cone, C. B., *The English Jacobins* (New York, 1968).
Greene, J. P. (ed.), *Colonies to Nation: 1763–1789* (New York, 1967).
Jensen, M. (ed.), *Tracts of the American Revolution* (Indianapolis, 1967).
Kramnick, I., *The Rage of Edmund Burke: Portrait of an Ambivalent Conservative* (New York, 1976).
Kurtz, S. G., and Hutson, J. H. (eds.), *Essays on the American Revolution* (New York, 1973).
Maier, P., *From Resistance to Revolution* (New York, 1974).
Thompson, E. P., *The Making of the English Working Class* (Penguin Books, Harmondsworth, 1968).

Opposite) *Facsimile title page of the first enlarged edition of* Common Sense, *1776*

COMMON SENSE;

ADDRESSED TO THE

INHABITANTS

OF

AMERICA,

On the following interesting

SUBJECTS:

I. Of the Origin and Design of Government in general, with concise Remarks on the English Constitution.

II. Of Monarchy and Hereditary Succession.

III. Thoughts on the present State of American Affairs.

IV. Of the present ability of America, with some miscellaneous Reflections.

A NEW EDITION, with several Additions in the Body of the Work. To which is Added an APPENDIX; together with an Address to the People called QUAKERS.

Man knows no Master save creating HEAVEN,
Or those whom choice and common Good ordain.
THOMSON.

PHILADELPHIA:

PRINTED and SOLD by W. and T. BRADFORD

M,DCC,LXXVI.

[PRICE ONE BRITISH SHILLING.]

INTRODUCTION

PERHAPS the sentiments contained in the following pages, are not yet sufficiently fashionable to procure them general favor; a long habit of not thinking a thing *wrong*, gives it a superficial appearance of being *right*, and raises at first a formidable outcry in defence of custom. But the tumult soon subsides. Time makes more converts than reason.

As a long and violent abuse of power, is generally the Means of calling the right of it in question (and in matters too which might never have been thought of, had not the Sufferers been aggravated into the inquiry) and as the K— of England had undertaken in his *own Right*, to support the Parliament in what he calls *Theirs*, and as the good people of this country are grievously oppressed by the combination, they have an undoubted privilege to inquire into the pretensions of both, and equally to reject the usurpation of either.

In the following sheets, the author hath studiously avoided every thing which is personal among ourselves. Compliments as well as censure to individuals make no part thereof. The wise, and the worthy, need not the triumph of a pamphlet; and those whose sentiments are injudicious, or unfriendly, will cease of themselves unless too much pains are bestowed upon their conversion.

The cause of America is in a great measure the cause of all mankind. Many circumstances hath, and will arise, which are not local, but universal, and through which the principles of all Lovers of Mankind are affected, and in the Event of which, their Affections are interested. The laying a Country desolate with Fire and Sword, declaring War against the natural rights of all Mankind, and extirpating the Defenders thereof from the Face of the Earth, is the

Concern of every Man to whom Nature hath given the Power of feeling; of which Class, regardless of Party Censure, is the

AUTHOR.

P.S. The Publication of this new Edition hath been delayed, with a View of taking notice (had it been necessary) of any Attempt to refute the Doctrine of Independance: As no Answer hath yet appeared, it is now presumed that none will, the Time needful for getting such a Performance ready for the Public being considerably past.

Who the Author of this Production is, is wholly unnecessary to the Public, as the Object for Attention is the *Doctrine itself,* not the *Man.* Yet it may not be unnecessary to say, That he is unconnected with any Party, and under no sort of Influence public or private, but the influence of reason and principle.

Philadelphia, February 14, 1776.

COMMON SENSE

OF THE ORIGIN AND DESIGN OF GOVERNMENT IN GENERAL. WITH CONCISE REMARKS ON THE ENGLISH CONSTITUTION.

SOME writers have so confounded society with government, as to leave little or no distinction between them; whereas they are not only different, but have different origins. Society is produced by our wants, and government by our wickedness; the former promotes our happiness *positively* by uniting our affections, the latter *negatively* by restraining our vices. The one encourages intercourse, the other creates distinctions. The first is a patron, the last a punisher.

Society in every state is a blessing, but government even in its best state is but a necessary evil; in its worst state an intolerable one; for when we suffer, or are exposed to the same miseries *by a government*, which we might expect in a country *without government*, our calamities is heightened by reflecting that we furnish the means by which we suffer. Government, like dress, is the badge of lost innocence; the palaces of kings are built on the ruins of the bowers of paradise. For were the impulses of conscience clear, uniform, and irresistibly obeyed, man would need no other lawgiver; but that not being the case, he finds it necessary to surrender up a part of his property to furnish means for the protection of the rest; and this he is induced to do by the same prudence which in every other case advises him out of two evils to choose the least. *Wherefore*, security being the true design and end of government, it unanswerably follows that whatever *form* thereof appears most likely to ensure it to us, with the least expence and greatest benefit, is preferable to all others.

In order to gain a clear and just idea of the design and end of government, let us suppose a small number of persons settled in some sequestered part of the earth, unconnected with the rest, they will then represent the first peopling of any country, or of the world. In this state of natural liberty, society will be their first thought. A thousand motives will excite them thereto, the strength of one man is so unequal to his wants, and his mind so unfitted for perpetual solitude, that he is soon obliged to seek assistance and relief of another, who in his turn requires the same. Four or five united would be able to raise a tolerable dwelling in the midst of a wilderness, but *one* man might labour out the common period of life without accomplishing any thing; when he had felled his timber he could not remove it, nor erect it after it was removed; hunger in the mean time would urge him from his work, and every different want call him a different way. Disease, nay even misfortune would be death, for though neither might be mortal, yet either would disable him from living, and reduce him to a state in which he might rather be said to perish than to die.

Thus necessity, like a gravitating power, would soon form our newly arrived emigrants into society, the reciprocal blessings of which, would supercede, and render the obligations of law and government unnecessary while they remained perfectly just to each other; but as nothing but heaven is impregnable to vice, it will unavoidably happen, that in proportion as they surmount the first difficulties of emigration, which bound them together in a common cause, they will begin to relax in their duty and attachment to each other; and this remissness, will point out the necessity, of establishing some form of government to supply the defect of moral virtue.

Some convenient tree will afford them a State-House, under the branches of which, the whole colony may assemble to deliberate on public matters. It is more than probable that their first laws will have the title only of REGULATIONS, and be enforced by no other penalty than public disesteem. In this first parliament every man, by natural right will have a seat.

But as the colony increases, the public concerns will increase likewise, and the distance at which the members may be separated, will render it too inconvenient for all of them to meet on every occasion as at first, when their number was small, their habitations near, and the public concerns few and trifling. This will point out the convenience of their consenting to leave the legislative part to be managed by a select number chosen from the whole body, who are supposed to have the same concerns at stake which those have who appointed them, and who will act in the same manner as the whole body would act were they present. If the colony continue increasing, it will become necessary to augment the number of the representatives, and that the interest of every part of the colony may be attended to, it will be found best to divide the whole into convenient parts, each part sending its proper number; and that the *elected* might never form to themselves an interest separate from the *electors*, prudence will point out the propriety of having elections often; because as the *elected* might by that means return and mix again with the general body of the *electors* in a few months, their fidelity to the public will be secured by the prudent reflexion of not making a rod for themselves. And as this frequent interchange will establish a common interest with every part of the community, they will mutually and naturally support each other, and on this (not on the unmeaning name of king) depends the *strength of government, and the happiness of the governed.*

Here then is the origin and rise of government; namely, a mode rendered necessary by the inability of moral virtue to govern the world; here too is the design and end of government, viz. freedom and security. And however our eyes may be dazzled with snow, or our ears deceived by sound; however prejudice may warp our wills, or interest darken our understanding, the simple voice of nature and of reason will say, it is right.

I draw my idea of the form of government from a principle in nature, which no art can overturn, viz. that the more simple any thing is, the less liable it is to be disordered, and the easier repaired when disordered; and with this maxim in view, I offer a few remarks on the so much boasted constitution of England. That it was noble for the dark and slavish times in which it was erected is granted. When the world was over-run with tyranny the least remove therefrom was a glorious rescue. But that it is imperfect, subject to convulsions, and incapable of producing what it seems to promise, is easily demonstrated.

Absolute governments (tho' the disgrace of human nature) have this advantage with them, that they are simple; if the people suffer, they know the head from which their suffering springs, know likewise the remedy, and are not bewildered by a variety of causes and cures. But the constitution of England is so exceedingly complex, that the nation may suffer for years together without being able to discover in which part the fault lies, some will say in one and some in another, and every political physician will advise a different medicine.

I know it is difficult to get over local or long standing prejudices, yet if we will suffer ourselves to examine the component parts of the English constitution, we shall find them to be the base remains of two ancient tyrannies, compounded with some new republican materials.

First. – The remains of monarchical tyranny in the person of the king.

Secondly. – The remains of aristocratical tyranny in the persons of the peers.

Thirdly. – The new republican materials, in the persons of the commons, on whose virtue depends the freedom of England.

The two first, by being hereditary, are independent of the people; wherefore in a *constitutional sense* they contribute nothing towards the freedom of the state.

To say that the constitution of England is a *union* of three powers reciprocally *checking* each other, is farcical, either the words have no meaning, or they are flat contradictions.

To say that the commons is a check upon the king, presupposes two things.

First. – That the king is not to be trusted without being looked after, or in other words, that a thirst for absolute power is the natural disease of monarchy.

Secondly. – That the commons, by being appointed for that purpose, are either wiser or more worthy of confidence than the crown.

But as the same constitution which gives the commons a power to check the king by withholding the supplies, gives afterwards the king a power to check the commons, by empowering him to reject their other bills; it again supposes that the king is wiser than those whom it has already supposed to be wiser than him. A mere absurdity!

There is something exceedingly ridiculous in the composition of monarchy; it first excludes a man from the means of information, yet empowers him to act in cases where the highest judgment is required. The state of a king shuts him from the world, yet the business of a king requires him to know it thoroughly; wherefore the different parts, unnaturally opposing and destroying each other, prove the whole character to be absurd and useless.

Some writers have explained the English constitution thus; the king, say they, is one, the people another; the peers are an house in behalf of the king; the commons in behalf of the people; but this hath all the distinctions of an house divided against itself; and though the expressions be pleasantly arranged, yet when examined they appear idle and ambiguous; and it will always happen, that the nicest construction that words are capable of, when applied to the description of some thing which either cannot exist, or is too incomprehensible to be within the compass of description, will be words of sound only, and though they may amuse the ear, they cannot inform the mind, for this explanation includes a previous question, viz. *How came the king by a power which the people are afraid to trust, and always obliged to check?* Such a power could not be the gift of a wise people, neither can any power, *which needs checking,* be from God; yet the provision, which the constitution makes, supposes such a power to exist.

But the provision is unequal to the task; the means either cannot or will not accomplish the end, and the whole affair is a *felo de se*; for as the greater weight will always carry up the less, and as all the wheels of a machine are put in motion by one, it only remains to know which power in the constitution has the most weight, for that will govern; and though the others, or a part of them, may clog, or, as the phrase is, check the rapidity of its motion, yet so long as they cannot stop it, their endeavours will be ineffectual; the first moving power will at last have its way, and what it wants in speed is supplied by time.

That the crown is this overbearing part in the English constitution needs not be mentioned, and that it derives its whole consequence merely from being the giver of places and pensions is self-evident, wherefore, though we have been wise enough to shut and lock a door against absolute monarchy, we at the same time have been foolish enough to put the crown in possession of the key.

The prejudice of Englishmen, in favour of their own government by king, lords, and commons, arises as much or more from national pride than reason. Individuals are undoubtedly safer in England than in some other countries, but the *will* of the king is as much the *law* of the land in Britain as in France, with this difference, that instead of proceeding directly from his mouth, it is handed to the people under the most formidable shape of an act of parliament. For the fate of Charles the First, hath only made kings more subtle – not more just.

Wherefore, laying aside all national pride and prejudice in favour of modes and forms, the plain truth is, that *it is wholly owing to the constitution of the people, and not to the constitution of the government* that the crown is not as oppressive in England as in Turkey.

An inquiry into the *constitutional errors* in the English form of government is at this time highly necessary; for as we are never in a proper condition of doing justice to others, while we continue under the influence of some leading partiality, so neither are we capable of doing it to ourselves while we remain fettered by any obstinate prejudice. And as a man, who is attached to a prostitute, is unfitted to choose or judge of a wife, so any prepossession in favour of a rotten constitution of government will disable us from discerning a good one.

OF MONARCHY AND HEREDITARY SUCCESSION.

MANKIND being originally equals in the order of creation, the equality could only be destroyed by some subsequent circumstance; the distinctions of rich, and poor, may in a great measure be accounted for, and that without having recourse to the harsh, ill-sounding names of oppression and avarice. Oppression is often the *consequence,* but seldom or never the *means* of riches; and though avarice will preserve a man from being necessitously poor, it generally makes him too timorous to be wealthy.

But there is another and greater distinction for which no truly natural or religious reason can be assigned, and that is, the distinction of men into KINGS and SUBJECTS. Male and female are the distinctions of nature, good and bad the distinctions of heaven; but how a race of men came into the world so exalted above the rest, and distinguished like some new species, is worth enquiring into, and whether they are the means of happiness or of misery to mankind.

In the early ages of the world, according to the scripture chronology, there were no kings; the consequence of which was there were no wars; it is the pride of kings which throw mankind into confusion. Holland without a king hath enjoyed more peace for this last century than any of the monarchial governments in Europe. Antiquity favors the same remark; for the quiet and rural lives of the first patriarchs hath a happy something in them, which vanishes away when we come to the history of Jewish royalty.

Government by kings was first introduced into the world by the Heathens, from whom the children of Israel copied the custom. It was the most prosperous invention the Devil ever set on foot for the promotion of idolatry. The Heathens paid divine honors to their deceased kings, and the christian world hath improved on the plan by doing the same to their living ones. How impious is the title of *sacred majesty* applied to a worm, who in the midst of his splendor is crumbling into dust.

As the exalting one man so greatly above the rest cannot be justified on the equal rights of nature, so neither can it be defended on the authority of scripture; for the will of the

Almighty, as declared by Gideon and the prophet Samuel, expressly disapproves of government by kings. All anti-monarchial parts of scripture have been very smoothly glossed over in monarchial governments, but they undoubtedly merit the attention of countries which have their governments yet to form. '*Render unto Cæsar the things which are Cæsar's*' is the scriptural doctrine of courts, yet it is no support of monarchial government, for the Jews at that time were without a king, and in a state of vassalage to the Romans.

Near three thousand years passed away from the Mosaic account of the creation, till the Jews under a national delusion requested a king. Till then their form of government (except in extraordinary cases, where the Almighty interposed) was a kind of republic administred by a judge and the elders of the tribes. Kings they had none, and it was held sinful to acknowledge any being under that title but the Lords of Hosts. And when a man seriously reflects on the idolatrous homage which is paid to the persons of Kings, he need not wonder, that the Almighty, ever jealous of his honor, should disapprove of a form of government which so impiously invades the prerogative of heaven.

Monarchy is ranked in scripture as one of the sins of the Jews, for which a curse in reserve is denounced against them. The history of that transaction is worth attending to.

The children of Israel being oppressed by the Midian-ites, Gideon marched against them with a small army, and victory, thro' the divine interposition, decided in his favour. The Jews elate with success, and attributing it to the generalship of Gideon, proposed making him a king, saying, *Rule thou over us, thou and thy son and thy son's son.* Here was temptation in its fullest extent; not a kingdom only, but an hereditary one, but Gideon in the piety of his soul replied, *I will not rule over you, neither shall my son rule over you,* THE LORD SHALL RULE OVER YOU. Words need not be more explicit; Gideon doth not *decline* the honor but denieth their right to give it; neither doth he compliment them with invented declarations of his thanks, but in the positive stile of a prophet charges them with disaffection to their proper sovereign, the King of Heaven.

About one hundred and thirty years after this, they fell again into the same error. The hankering which the Jews had for the idolatrous customs of the Heathens, is something exceedingly unaccountable; but so it was, that laying hold of the misconduct of Samuel's two sons, who were entrusted with some secular concerns, they came in an abrupt and clamourous manner to Samuel, saying, *Behold thou art old, and thy sons walk not in thy ways, now make us a king to judge us like all the other nations.* And here we cannot but observe that their motives were bad, viz. that they might be *like* unto other nations, i. e. the Heathens, whereas their true glory laid in being as much *unlike* them as possible. *But the thing displeased Samuel when they said, give us a king to judge us*; *and Samuel prayed unto the Lord, and the Lord said unto Samuel, Hearken unto the voice of the people in all that they say unto thee, for they have not rejected thee, but they have rejected me,* THAT I SHOULD NOT REIGN OVER THEM. *According to all the works which they have done since the day that I brought them up out of Egypt, even unto this day; wherewith they have forsaken me and served other Gods; so do they also unto thee. Now therefore hearken unto their voice, howbeit, protest solemnly unto them and shew them the manner of the king that shall reign over them,* i. e. not of any particular king, but the general manner of the kings of the earth, whom Israel was so eagerly copying after. And notwithstanding the great distance of time and difference of manners, the character is still in fashion, *And Samuel told all the words of the Lord unto the people, that asked of him a king. And he said, This shall be the manner of the king that shall reign over you; he will take your sons and appoint them for himself for his chariots, and to be his horse-men, and some shall run before his chariots* (this description agrees with the present mode of impressing men) *and he will appoint him captains over thousands and captains over fifties, and will set them to ear his ground and to reap his harvest, and to make his instruments of war, and instruments of his chariots; and he will take your daughters to be confectionaries and to be cooks and to be bakers* (this describes the expence and luxury as well as the oppression of kings) *and he will take your fields and your olive yards, even the best of them, and give them to his servants; and he will take the tenth of your seed, and of your vineyards, and give them to his officers and to his servants* (by which we see that bribery, corruption, and favoritism are the standing vices of kings) *and he will take the tenth of your men servants, and your maid servants, and your goodliest young men and your asses, and put them to his work; and he will take the tenth of your sheep, and ye shall be his servants, and ye shall cry out in that day because of your king which ye shall have chosen,* AND THE LORD WILL NOT HEAR YOU IN THAT DAY. This accounts for the continuation of monarchy; neither do the characters of the few good kings which have lived since, either sanctify the title, or blot out the sinfulness of the origin; the high encomium given of David takes no notice of him *officially as a king,* but only as a *man* after God's own heart. *Nevertheless the People refused to obey the voice of Samuel, and they said, Nay, but we will have a king over us, that we may be like all the nations, and that our king may judge us, and go out before us and fight our battles.* Samuel continued to reason with them, but to no purpose; he set before them their ingratitude, but all would not avail; and seeing them fully bent on their folly, he cried out, *I will call unto the Lord, and he shall send thunder and rain* (which then was a punishment, being the time of wheat harvest) *that ye may perceive and see that your wickedness is great which ye have done in the sight of the Lord,* IN ASKING YOU A KING. *So Samuel called unto the Lord, and the Lord sent*

*thunder and rain that day, and all the people greatly feared the
Lord and Samuel. And all the people said unto Samuel, Pray for
thy servants unto the Lord thy God that we die not, for* WE
HAVE ADDED UNTO OUR SINS THIS EVIL, TO ASK A
KING. These portions of scripture are direct and positive.
They admit of no equivocal construction. That the
Almighty hath here entered his protest against monarchial
government is true, or the scripture is false. And a man
hath good reason to believe that there is as much of king-
craft, as priest-craft in withholding the scripture from the
public in Popish countries. For monarchy in every
instance is the Popery of government.

To the evil of monarchy we have added that of hereditary
succession; and as the first is a degredation and lessening of
ourselves, so the second, claimed as a matter of right, is an
insult and an imposition on posterity. For all men being
originally equals, no *one* by *birth* could have a right to set up
his own family in perpetual preference to all others for
ever, and though himself might deserve *some* decent degree
of honors of his contemporaries, yet his descendants might
be far too unworthy to inherit them. One of the strongest
natural proofs of the folly of hereditary right in kings, is,
that nature disapproves it, otherwise she would not so
frequently turn it into ridicule by giving mankind an *ass for
a lion*.

Secondly, as no man at first could possess any other
public honors than were bestowed upon him, so the givers
of those honors could have no power to give away the
right of posterity, and though they might say 'We choose
you for *our* head,' they could not, without manifest
injustice to their children, say 'that your children and your
children's children shall reign over *ours* for ever.' Because
such an unwise, unjust, unnatural compact might (perhaps) in the next succession put them under the government of a rogue or a fool. Most wise men, in their private

sentiments, have ever treated hereditary right with contempt; yet it is one of those evils, which when once established is not easily removed; many submit from fear, others from superstition, and the more powerful part shares with the king the plunder of the rest.

This is supposing the present race of kings in the world to have had an honourable origin; whereas it is more than probable, that could we take off the dark covering of antiquity, and trace them to their first rise, that we should find the first of them nothing better than the principal ruffian of some restless gang, whose savage manners or pre-eminence in subtilty obtained him the title of chief among plunderers; and who by increasing in power, and extending his depredations, over-awed the quiet and defenceless to purchase their safety by frequent contributions. Yet his electors could have no idea of giving hereditary right to his descendants, because such a perpetual exclusion of themselves was incompatible with the free and unrestrained principles they professed to live by. Wherefore, hereditary succession in the early ages of monarchy could not take place as a matter of claim, but as something casual or complimental; but as few or no records were extant in those days, and traditionary history stuffed with fables, it was very easy, after the lapse of a few generations, to trump up some superstitious tale, conveniently timed, Mahomet like, to cram hereditary right down the throats of the vulgar. Perhaps the disorders which threatened, or seemed to threaten on the decease of a leader and the choice of a new one (for elections among ruffians could not be very orderly) induced many at first to favor hereditary pretentions; by which means it happened, as it hath happened since, that what at first was submitted to as a convenience, was afterwards claimed as a right.

England, since the conquest, hath known some few good monarchs, but groaned beneath a much larger number of bad ones, yet no man in his senses can say that their claim under William the Conqueror is a very honorable one. A French bastard landing with an armed banditti, and establishing himself king of England against the consent of the natives, is in plain terms a very paltry rascally original. – It certainly hath no divinity in it. However, it is needless to spend much time in exposing the folly of hereditary right, if there are any so weak as to believe it, let them promiscuously worship the ass and lion, and welcome. I shall neither copy their humility, nor disturb their devotion.

Yet I should be glad to ask how they suppose kings came at first? The question admits but of three answers, viz. either by lot, by election, or by usurpation. If the first king was taken by lot, it establishes a precedent for the next, which excludes hereditary succession. Saul was by lot yet the succession was not hereditary, neither does it appear from that transaction there was any intention it ever should. If the first king of any country was by election, that likewise establishes a precedent for the next; for to say, that the *right* of all future generations is taken away, by the act of the first electors, in their choice not only of a king, but of a family of kings for ever, hath no parallel in or out of scripture but the doctrine of original sin, which supposes the free will of all men lost in Adam; and from such comparison, and it will admit of no other, hereditary succession can derive no glory. For as in Adam all sinned, and as in the first electors all men obeyed; as in the one all mankind were subjected to Satan, and in the other to Sovereignty; as our innocence was lost in the first, and our authority in the last; and as both disable us from re-assuming some former state and privilege, it unanswerably follows that original sin and hereditary succession are parallels. Dishonourable rank! Inglorious connexion! Yet the most subtile sophist cannot produce a juster simile.

As to usurpation, no man will be so hardy as to defend it; and that William the Conqueror was an usurper is a fact not to be contradicted. The plain truth is, that the antiquity of English monarchy will not bear looking into.

But it is not so much the absurdity as the evil of hereditary succession which concerns mankind. Did it ensure a race of good and wise men it would have the seal of divine authority, but as it opens a door to the *foolish*, the *wicked*, and the *improper*, it hath in it the nature of oppression. Men who look upon themselves born to reign, and others to obey, soon grow insolent; selected from the rest of mankind their minds are early poisoned by importance; and the world they act in differs so materially from the world at large, that they have but little opportunity of knowing its true interests, and when they succeed to the government are frequently the most ignorant and unfit of any throughout the dominions.

Another evil which attends hereditary succession is, that the throne is subject to be possessed by a minor at any age; all which time the regency, acting under the cover of a king, have every opportunity and inducement to betray their trust. The same national misfortune happens, when a king worn out with age and infirmity, enters the last stage of human weakness. In both these cases the public becomes a prey to every miscreant, who can tamper successfully with the follies either of age or infancy.

The most plausible plea, which hath ever been offered in favour of hereditary succession, is, that it preserves a nation from civil wars; and were this true, it would be weighty; whereas, it is the most barefaced falsity ever imposed upon mankind. The whole history of England disowns the fact. Thirty kings and two minors have reigned in that distracted kingdom since the conquest, in which time there have been (including the Revolution) no less than eight civil wars and nineteen rebellions. Wherefore instead of making for peace, it makes against it, and destroys the very foundation it seems to stand on.

The contest for monarchy and succession, between the houses of York and Lancaster, laid England in a scene of blood for many years. Twelve pitched battles, besides skirmishes and sieges, were fought between Henry and Edward. Twice was Henry prisoner to Edward, who in his turn was prisoner to Henry. And so uncertain is the fate of war and the temper of a nation, when nothing but personal matters are the ground of a quarrel, that Henry was taken in triumph from a prison to a palace, and Edward obliged to fly from a palace to a foreign land; yet, as sudden transitions of temper are seldom lasting, Henry in his turn was driven from the throne, and Edward recalled to succeed him. The parliament always following the strongest side.

This contest began in the reign of Henry the Sixth, and was not entirely extinguished till Henry the Seventh, in whom the families were united. Including a period of 67 years, viz. from 1422 to 1489.

In short, monarchy and succession have laid (not this or that kingdom only) but the world in blood and ashes. 'Tis a form of government which the word of God bears testimony against, and blood will attend it.

If we inquire into the business of a king, we shall find that in some countries they have none; and after sauntering away their lives without pleasure to themselves or advantage to the nation, withdraw from the scene, and leave their successors to tread the same idle round. In absolute monarchies the whole weight of business civil and military, lies on the king; the children of Israel in their request for a king, urged this plea 'that he may judge us, and go out before us and fight our battles.' But in countries where he is neither a judge nor a general, as in E——d, a man would be puzzled to know what *is* his business.

The nearer any government approaches to a republic the

less business there is for a king. It is somewhat difficult to find a proper name for the government of E—. Sir William Meredith calls it a republic; but in its present state it is unworthy of the name, because the corrupt influence of the crown, by having all the places in its disposal, hath so effectually swallowed up the power, and eaten out the virtue of the house of commons (the republican part in the constitution) that the government of England is nearly as monarchical as that of France or Spain. Men fall out with names without understanding them. For it is the republican and not the monarchical part of the constitution of England which Englishmen glory in, viz. the liberty of choosing an house of commons from out of their own body – and it is easy to see that when the republican virtue fails, slavery ensues. Why is the constitution of E—d sickly, but because monarchy hath poisoned the republic, the crown hath engrossed the commons?

In England a k— hath little more to do than to make war and give away places; which in plain terms, is to impoverish the nation and set it together by the ears. A pretty business indeed for a man to be allowed eight hundred thousand sterling a year for, and worshipped into the bargain! Of more worth is one honest man to society, and in the sight of God, than all the crowned ruffians that ever lived.

THOUGHTS ON THE PRESENT STATE OF
AMERICAN AFFAIRS.

In the following pages I offer nothing more than simple facts, plain arguments, and common sense; and have no other preliminaries to settle with the reader, than that he will divest himself of prejudice and prepossession, and suffer his reason and his feelings to determine for themselves; that he will put *on*, or rather that he will not put *off*, the true character of a man, and generously enlarge his views beyond the present day.

Volumes have been written on the subject of the struggle between England and America. Men of all ranks have embarked in the controversy, from different motives, and with various designs; but all have been ineffectual, and the period of debate is closed. Arms, as the last resource, decide the contest; the appeal was the choice of the king, and the continent hath accepted the challenge.

It hath been reported of the late Mr Pelham (who tho' an able minister was not without his faults) that on his being attacked in the house of commons, on the score, that his measures were only of a temporary kind, replied, '*they will last my time.*' Should a thought so fatal and unmanly possess the colonies in the present contest, the name of ancestors will be remembered by future generations with detestation.

The sun never shined on a cause of greater worth. 'Tis not the affair of a city, a country, a province, or a kingdom, but of a continent – of at least one eighth part of the habitable globe. 'Tis not the concern of a day, a year, or an age; posterity are virtually involved in the contest, and will be more or less affected, even to the end of time, by the proceedings now. Now is the seed time of continental union, faith and honor. The least fracture now will be like a name engraved with the point of a pin on the tender rind of a young oak; the wound will enlarge with the tree, and posterity read it in full grown characters.

By referring the matter from argument to arms, a new æra for politics is struck; a new method of thinking hath arisen. All plans, proposals, &c. prior to the nineteenth of April, *i. e.* to the commencement of hostilities, are like the almanacks of the last year; which, though proper then, are superceded and useless now. Whatever was advanced by the advocates on either side of the question then, terminated in one and the same point, viz. a union with Great Britain; the only difference between the parties was the method of effecting it; the one proposing force, the other friendship; but it hath so far happened that the first hath failed, and the second hath withdrawn her influence.

As much hath been said of the advantages of reconciliation, which, like an agreeable dream, hath passed away and left us as we were, it is but right, that we should examine the contrary side of the argument, and inquire into some of the many material injuries which these colonies sustain, and always will sustain, by being connected with, and dependant on Great Britain. To examine that connexion and dependance, on the principles of nature and common sense, to see what we have to trust to, if separated, and what we are to expect, if dependant.

I have heard it asserted by some, that as America hath flourished under her former connexion with Great-Britain, that the same connexion is necessary towards her future happiness, and will always have the same effect. Nothing can be more fallacious than this kind of argument. We may as well assert, that because a child has thrived upon milk, that it is never to have meat; or that the first twenty years of our lives is to become a precedent for the next twenty. But even this is admitting more than is true, for I answer roundly, that America would have flourished as much, and probably much more, had no European power had any thing to do with her. The commerce by which she hath enriched herself are the necessaries of life, and will always have a market while eating is the custom of Europe.

But she has protected us, say some. That she hath engrossed us is true, and defended the continent at our expence as well as her own is admitted, and she would have defended Turkey from the same motive, viz. the sake of trade and dominion.

Alas, we have been long led away by ancient prejudices,

and made large sacrifices to superstition. We have boasted the protection of Great-Britain, without considering, that her motive was *interest* not *attachment*; that she did not protect us from *our enemies* on *our account,* but from *her enemies* on *her own account,* from those who had no quarrel with us on any *other account,* and who will always be our enemies on the *same account.* Let Britain wave her pretensions to the continent, or the continent throw off the dependance, and we should be at peace with France and Spain were they at war with Britain. The miseries of Hanover last war ought to warn us against connexions.

It hath lately been asserted in parliament, that the colonies have no relation to each other but through the parent country, *i. e.* that Pensylvania and the Jerseys, and so on for the rest, are sister colonies by the way of England; this is certainly a very round-about way of proving relationship, but it is the nearest and only true way of proving enemyship, if I may so call it. France and Spain never were, nor perhaps ever will be our enemies as *Americans,* but as our being the *subjects of Great Britain.*

But Britain is the parent country, say some. Then the more shame upon her conduct. Even brutes do not devour their young, nor savages make war upon their families; wherefore the assertion, if true, turns to her reproach; but it happens not to be true, or only partly so, and the phrase *parent* or *mother country* hath been jesuitically adopted by the — and his parasites, with a low papistical design of gaining an unfair bias on the credulous weakness of our minds. Europe, and not England, is the parent country of America. This new world hath been the asylum for the persecuted lovers of civil and religious liberty from *every part* of Europe. Hither have they fled, not from the tender embraces of the mother, but from the cruelty of the monster; and it is so far true of England, that the same tyranny which drove the first emigrants from home, pursues their descendants still.

In this extensive quarter of the globe, we forget the narrow limits of three hundred and sixty miles (the extent of England) and carry our friendship on a larger scale; we claim brotherhood with eve European christian, and triumph in the generosity of the sentiment.

It is pleasant to observe by what regular gradations we surmount the force of local prejudice, as we enlarge our acquaintance with the world. A man born in any town in England divided into parishes, will naturally associate most with his fellow parishioners (because their interests in many cases will be common) and distinguish him by the name of *neighbour*; if he meet him but a few miles from home, he drops the narrow idea of a street, and salutes him by the name of *townsman*; if he travels out of the county, and meet him in any other, he forgets the minor divisions of street and town, and calls him *countryman, i.e. countyman*; but if in their foreign excursions they should associate in France or any other part of *Europe*, their local remembrance would be enlarged into that of *Englishmen*. And by a just parity of reasoning, all Europeans meeting in America, or any other quarter of the globe, are *countrymen*; for England, Holland, Germany, or Sweden, when compared with the whole, stand in the same places on the larger scale, which the divisions of street, town, and county do on the smaller ones; distinctions too limited for continental minds. Not one third of the inhabitants, even of this province, are of English descent. Wherefore I reprobate the phrase of parent or mother country applied to England only, as being false, selfish, narrow and ungenerous.

But admitting that we were all of English descent, what does it amount to? Nothing. Britain, being now an open enemy, extinguishes every other name and title: And to say that reconciliation is our duty, is truly farcical. The first king of England, of the present line (William the Conqueror) was a Frenchman, and half the peers of England are descendants from the same country; wherefore by the same method of reasoning, England ought to be governed by France.

Much hath been said of the united strength of Britain and the colonies, that in conjunction they might bid defiance to the world. But this is mere presumption; the fate of war is uncertain, neither do the expressions mean any thing; for this continent would never suffer itself to be drained of inhabitants to support the British arms in either Asia, Africa, or Europe.

Besides, what have we to do with setting the world at defiance? Our plan is commerce, and that, well attended to, will secure us the peace and friendship of all Europe; because it is the interest of all Europe to have America a *free port*. Her trade will always be a protection, and her barrenness of gold and silver secure her from invaders.

I challenge the warmest advocate for reconciliation, to shew, a single advantage that this continent can reap, by being connected with Great Britain. I repeat the challenge, not a single advantage is derived. Our corn will fetch its price in any market in Europe, and our imported goods must be paid for buy them where we will.

But the injuries and disadvantages we sustain by that connection, are without number; and our duty to mankind at large, as well as to ourselves, instruct us to renounce the alliance: Because, any submission to, or dependance on Great Britain, tends directly to involve this continent in European wars and quarrels; and sets us at variance with nations, who would otherwise seek our friendship, and against whom, we have neither anger nor complaint As Europe is our market for trade, we ought to form no partial connection with any part of it. It is the true interest of America to steer clear of European contentions, which she never can do, while by her dependance on Britain, she is made the make-weight in the scale of British politics.

Europe is too thickly planted with kingdoms to be long at peace, and whenever a war breaks out between England and any foreign power, the trade of America goes to ruin, *because of her connection with Britain*. The next war may not turn out like the last, and should it not, the advocates for reconciliation now will be wishing for separation then, because, neutrality in that case, would be a safer convoy than a man of war. Every thing that is right or natural pleads for separation. The blood of the slain, the weeping voice of nature cries, 'TIS TIME TO PART. Even the distance at which the Almighty hath placed England and America, is a strong and natural proof, that the authority of the one, over the other, was never the design of Heaven. The time likewise at which the continent was discovered, adds weight to the argument, and the manner in which it was peopled encreases the force of it. The reformation was preceded by the discovery of America, as if the Almighty graciously meant to open a sanctuary to the persecuted in future years, when home should afford neither friendship nor safety.

The authority of Great-Britain over this continent, is a form of government, which sooner or later must have an end: And a serious mind can draw no true pleasure by looking forward, under the painful and positive conviction, that what he calls 'the present constitution' is merely temporary. As parents, we can have no joy, knowing that *this government* is not sufficiently lasting to ensure any thing which we may bequeath to posterity: And by a plain method of argument, as we are running the next generation into debt, we ought to do the work of it, otherwise we use them meanly and pitifully. In order to discover the line of our duty rightly, we should take our children in our hand, and fix our station a few years farther into life; that eminence will present a prospect, which a few present fears and prejudices conceal from our sight.

Though I would carefully avoid giving unnecessary offence, yet I am inclined to believe, that all those who espouse the doctrine of reconciliation, may be included within the following descriptions. Interested men, who are not to be trusted; weak men who *cannot* see; prejudiced men who *will not* see; and a certain set of moderate men, who think better of the European world than it deserves; and this last class by an ill-judged deliberation, will be the cause of more calamities to this continent than all the other three.

It is the good fortune of many to live distant from the scene of sorrow; the evil is not sufficiently brought to *their* doors to make *them* feel the precariousness with which all American property is possessed. But let our imaginations transport us for a few moments to Boston, that seat of wretchedness will teach us wisdom, and instruct us for ever to renounce a power in whom we can have no trust. The inhabitants of that unfortunate city, who but a few months ago were in ease and affluence, have now no other alternative than to stay and starve, or turn out to beg. Endangered by the fire of their friends if they continue within the city, and plundered by the soldiery if they leave it. In their present condition they are prisoners without the hope of redemption, and in a general attack for their relief, they would be exposed to the fury of both armies.

Men of passive tempers look somewhat lightly over the offences of Britain, and, still hoping for the best, are apt to call out, '*Come we shall be friends again for all this.*' But examine the passions and feelings of mankind. Bring the doctrine of reconciliation to the touchstone of nature, and then tell me, whether you can hereafter love, honour, and faithfully serve the power that hath carried fire and sword into your land? If you cannot do all these, then are you only deceiving yourselves, and by your delay bringing ruin upon posterity. Your future connection with Britain, whom you can neither love nor honour, will be forced and unnatural, and being formed only on the plan of present convenience, will in a little time fall into a relapse more wretched than the first. But if you say, you can still pass the violations over, then I ask, Hath your house been burnt? Hath your property been destroyed before your face? Are your wife and children destitute of a bed to lie on, or bread to live on? Have you lost a parent or a child by their hands, and yourself the ruined and wretched survivor? If you have not, then are you not a judge of those who have. But if you have, and can still shake hands with the murderers, then are you unworthy the name of husband, father, friend, or lover, and whatever may be your rank or title in life, you have the heart of a coward, and the spirit of a sycophant.

This is not inflaming or exaggerating matters, but trying them by those feelings and affections which nature justifies, and without which, we should be incapable of discharging the social duties of life, or enjoying the felicities of it. I mean not to exhibit horror for the purpose of provoking revenge, but to awaken us from fatal and unmanly slumbers, that we may pursue determinately some fixed object. It is not in the power of Britain or of Europe to conquer America, if she do not conquer herself by *delay* and *timidity*. The present winter is worth an age if rightly employed, but if lost or neglected, the whole continent will partake of the misfortune; and there is no punishment which that man will not deserve, be he who, or what, or where he will, that may be the means of sacrificing a season so precious and useful.

It is repugnant to reason, to the universal order of things, to all examples from the former ages, to suppose, that this continent can longer remain subject to any external power. The most sanguine in Britain does not think so.

The utmost stretch of human wisdom cannot, at this time compass a plan short of separation, which can promise the continent even a year's security. Reconciliation is was a falacious dream. Nature hath deserted the connexion, and Art cannot supply her place. For, as Milton wisely expresses, 'never can true reconcilement grow where wounds of deadly hate have pierced so deep.'

Every quiet method for peace hath been ineffectual. Our prayers have been rejected with disdain; and only tended to convince us, that nothing flatters vanity, or confirms obstinacy in Kings more than repeated petitioning – and nothing hath contributed more than that very measure to make the Kings of Europe absolute: Witness Denmark and Sweden. Wherefore since nothing but blows will do, for God's sake, let us come to a final separation, and not leave the next generation to be cutting throats, under the violated unmeaning names of parent and child.

To say, they will never attempt it again is idle and visionary, we thought so at the repeal of the stamp-act, yet a year or two undeceived us; as well we may suppose that nations, which have been once defeated, will never renew the quarrel.

As to government matters, it is not in the power of Britain to do this continent justice: The business of it will soon be too weighty, and intricate, to be managed with any tolerable degree of convenience, by a power, so distant from us, and so very ignorant of us; for if they cannot conquer us, they cannot govern us. To be always running three or four thousand miles with a tale or a petition, waiting four or five months for an answer, which when obtained requires five or six more to explain it in, will in a few years be looked upon as folly and childishness – There was a time when it was proper, and there is a proper time for it to cease.

Small islands not capable of protecting themselves, are the proper objects for kingdoms to take under their care;

but there is something very absurd, in supposing a continent to be perpetually governed by an island. In no instance hath nature made the satellite larger than its primary planet, and as England and America, with respect to each other, reverses the common order of nature, it is evident they belong to different systems: England to Europe, America to itself.

I am not induced by motives of pride, party, or resentment to espouse the doctrine of separation and independance; I am clearly, positively, and conscientiously persuaded that it is the true interest of this continent to be so; that every thing short of *that* is mere patchwork, that it can afford no lasting felicity, – that it is leaving the sword to our children, and shrinking back at a time, when, a little more, a little farther, would have rendered this continent the glory of the earth.

As Britain hath not manifested the least inclination towards a compromise, we may be assured that no terms can be obtained worthy the acceptance of the continent, or any ways equal to the expence of blood and treasure we have been already put to.

The object contended for, ought always to bear some just proportion to the expence. The removal of N—, or the whole detestable junto, is a matter unworthy the millions we have expended. A temporary stoppage of trade, was an inconvenience, which would have sufficiently ballanced the repeal of all the acts complained of, had such repeals been obtained; but if the whole continent must take up arms, if every man must be a soldier, it is scarcely worth out while to fight against a contemptible ministry only. Dearly, dearly, do we pay for the repeal of the acts, if that is all we fight for; for in a just estimation, it is as great a folly to pay a Bunker-hill price for law, as for land. As I have always considered the independancy of this continent, as an event, which sooner or later must arrive, so from the late rapid progress of the continent to maturity, the event could not be far off. Wherefore, on the breaking out of hostilities, it was not worth the while to have disputed a matter, which time would have finally redressed, unless we meant to be in earnest; otherwise, it is like wasting an estate on a suit at law, to regulate the trespasses of a tenant, whose lease is just expiring. No man was a warmer wisher for reconciliation than myself, before the fatal nineteenth of April 1775*, but the moment the event of that day was made known, I rejected the hardened, sullen tempered Pharoah of — for ever; and disdain the wretch, that with the pretended title of FATHER OF HIS PEOPLE can unfeelingly hear of their slaughter, and composedly sleep with their blood upon his soul.

But admitting that matters were now made up, what would be the event? I answer, the ruin of the continent. And that for several reasons.

First. The powers of governing still remaining in the hands of the k—, he will have a negative over the whole legislation of this continent. And as he hath shewn himself such an inveterate enemy to liberty, and discovered such a thirst for arbitrary power; is he, or is he not, a proper man to say to these colonies, '*You shall make no laws but what I please.*' And is there any inhabitants in America so ignorant, as not to know, that according to what is called the *present constitution,* that this continent can make no laws but what the king gives leave to; and is there any man so unwise, as not to see, that (considering what has happened) he will suffer no Law to be made here, but such as suit his purpose. We may be as effectually enslaved by the want of laws in America, as by submitting to laws made for us in England. After matters are made up (as it is called) can there be any doubt but the whole power of the crown will

---

* Massacre at Lexington.

be exerted, to keep this continent as low and humble as possible? Instead of going forward we shall go backward, or be perpetually quarrelling or ridiculously petitioning. – We are already greater than the king wishes us to be, and will he not hereafter endeavour to make us less? To bring the matter to one point. Is the power who is jealous of our prosperity, a proper power to govern us? Whoever says *No* to this question is an *independant,* for independancy means no more, than, whether we shall make our own laws, or, whether the —, the greatest enemy this continent hath, or can have, shall tell us '*there shall be no laws but such as I like.*'

But the k— you will say has a negative in England; the people there can make no laws without his consent. In point of right and good order, there is something very ridiculous, that a youth of twenty-one (which hath often happened) shall say to several millions of people, older and wiser than himself, I forbid this or that act of yours to be law. But in this place I decline this sort of reply, tho' I will never cease to expose the absurdity of it, and only answer, that England being the king's residence, and America not so, makes quite another case. The k—'s negative *here* is ten times more dangerous and fatal than it can be in England, for *there* he will scarcely refuse his consent to a bill for putting England into as strong a state of defence as possible, and in America he would never suffer such a bill to be passed.

America is only a secondary object in the system of British politics. England consults the good of *this* country, no farther than it answers her *own* purpose. Wherefore, her own interest leads her to suppress the growth of *ours* in every case which doth not promote her advantage, or in the least interfere with it. A pretty state we should soon be in under such a second-hand government, considering what has happened! Men do not change from enemies to friends by the alteration of a name: And in order to shew that reconciliation *now* is a dangerous doctrine, I affirm, *that it*

*would be policy in the k— at this time, to repeal the acts for the
sake of reinstating himself in the government of the provinces*; in
order, that HE MAY ACCOMPLISH BY CRAFT AND
SUBTILTY, IN THE LONG RUN, WHAT HE CANNOT DO
BY FORCE AND VIOLENCE IN THE SHORT ONE.
Reconciliation and ruin are nearly related.

Secondly, That as even the best terms, which we can
expect to obtain, can amount to no more than a temporary
expedient, or a kind of government by guardianship,
which can last no longer than till the colonies come of age,
so the general face and state of things, in the interim, will be
unsettled and unpromising. Emigrants of property will
not choose to come to a country whose form of government hangs but by a thread, and who is every day tottering
on the brink of commotion and disturbance; and numbers
of the present inhabitants would lay hold of the interval, to
dispose of their effects, and quit the continent.

But the most powerful of all arguments, is, that nothing
but independance, i. e. a continental form of government,
can keep the peace of the continent and preserve it inviolate
from civil wars. I dread the event of a reconciliation with
Britain now, as it is more than probable, that it will be
followed by a revolt somewhere or other, the consequences
of which may be far more fatal than all the malice of
Britain.

Thousands are already ruined by British barbarity;
(thousands more will probably suffer the same fate.) Those
men have other feelings than us who have nothing suffered.
All they *now* possess is liberty, what they before enjoyed is
sacrificed to its service, and having nothing more to lose,
they disdain submission. Besides, the general temper of the
colonies, towards a British government, will be like that of
a youth, who is nearly out of his time, they will care very
little about her. And a government which cannot preserve
the peace, is no government at all, and in that case we pay

our money for nothing; and pray what is it that Britain can do, whose power will be wholly on paper, should a civil tumult break out the very day after reconciliation? I have heard some men say, many of whom I believe spoke without thinking, that they dreaded an independance, fearing that it would produce civil wars. It is but seldom that our first thoughts are truly correct, and that is the case here; for there are ten times more to dread from a patched up connexion than from independance. I make the sufferers case my own, and I protest, that were I driven from house and home, my property destroyed, and my circumstances ruined, that as man, sensible of injuries, I could never relish the doctrine of reconciliation, or consider myself bound thereby.

The colonies have manifested such a spirit of good order and obedience to continental government, as is sufficient to make every reasonable person easy and happy on that head. No man can assign the least pretence for his fears, on any other grounds, that such as are truly childish and ridiculous, that one colony will be striving for superiority over another.

Where there are no distinctions there can be no superiority, perfect equality affords no temptation. The republics of Europe are all (and we may say always) in peace. Holland and Swisserland are without wars, foreign or domestic: Monarchical governments, it is true, are never long at rest; the crown itself is a temptation to enterprizing ruffians at *home*; and that degree of pride and insolence ever attendant on regal authority, swells into a rupture with foreign powers, in instances, where a republican government, by being formed on more natural principles, would negociate the mistake.

If there is any true cause of fear respecting independance, it is because no plan is yet laid down. Men do not see their way out – Wherefore, as an opening into that business, I offer the following hints; at the same time modestly affirming, that I have no other opinion of them myself, than that they may be the means of giving rise to something better. Could the straggling thoughts of individuals be collected, they would frequently form materials for wise and able men to improve to useful matter.

LET the assemblies be annual, with a President only. The representation more equal. Their business wholly domestic, and subject to the authority of a Continental Congress.

Let each colony be divided into six, eight, or ten, convenient districts, each district to send a proper number of delegates to Congress, so that each colony send at least thirty. The whole number in Congress will be at least 390. Each Congress to sit and to choose a president by the following method. When the delegates are met, let a colony be taken from the whole thirteen colonies by lot, after which let the whole Congress choose (by ballot) a president from out of the delegates of *that* province. In the next Congress, let a colony be taken by lot from twelve only, omitting that colony from which the president was taken in the former Congress, and so proceeding on till the whole thirteen shall have had their proper rotation. And in order that nothing may pass into a law but what is satisfactorily just, not less than three fifths of the Congress to be called a majority. – He that will promote discord, under a government so equally formed as this, would join Lucifer in his revolt.

But as there is a peculiar delicacy, from whom, or in what manner, this business must first arise, and as it seems most agreeable and consistent, that it should come from some intermediate body between the governed and the governors, that is between the Congress and the people, let a CONTINENTAL CONFERENCE be held, in the following manner, and for the following purpose.

A committee of twenty-six members of Congress, viz. two for each colony. Two members for each house of assembly, or Provincial convention; and five representatives of the people at large, to be chosen in the capital city or town of each province, for, and in behalf of the whole province, by as many qualified voters as shall think proper to attend from all parts of the province for that purpose; or, if more convenient, the representatives may be chosen in two or three of the most populous parts thereof. In this conference, thus assembled, will be united, the two grand principles of business, *knowledge* and *power*. The members of Congress, Assemblies, or Conventions, by having had experience in national concerns, will be able and useful counsellors, and the whole, being impowered by the people will have a truly legal authority.

The conferring members being met, let their business be to frame a CONTINENTAL CHARTER, or Charter of the United Colonies; (answering to what is called the Magna Charta of England) fixing the number and manner of choosing members of Congress, members of Assembly, with their date of sitting, and drawing the line of business and jurisdiction between them: (Always remembering, that our strength is continental, not provincial:) Securing freedom and property to all men, and above all things the free exercise of religion, according to the dictates of conscience; with such other matter as is necessary for a charter to contain. Immediately after which, the said conference to dissolve, and the bodies which shall be chosen conformable to the said charter, to be the legislators and governors of this continent for the time being: Whose peace and happiness, may God preserve, Amen.

Should any body of men be hereafter delegated for this or some similar purpose, I offer them the following extracts from that wise observer on governments *Dragonetti*. 'The science' says he, 'of the politician

'consists in fixing the true point of happiness and freedom.
'Those men would deserve the gratitude of ages, who
'should discover a mode of government that contained the
'greatest sum of individual happiness, with the least
'national expence.

> *Dragonetti on Virtue and Rewards.'*

But where says some is the King of America? I'll tell
you Friend, he reigns above, and doth not make havock of
mankind like the Royal — of Britain. Yet that we may not
appear to be defective even in earthly honors, let a day be
solemnly set apart for proclaiming the charter; let it be
brought forth placed on the divine law, the word of God;
let a crown be placed thereon, by which the world may
know, that so far as we approve of monarchy, that in
America THE LAW IS KING. For as in absolute governments the King is law, so in free countries the law *ought* to
be King; and there ought to be no other. But lest any ill use
should afterwards arise, let the crown at the conclusion of
the ceremony be demolished, and scattered among the
people whose right it is.

A government of our own is our natural right: And
when a man seriously reflects on the precariousness of
human affairs, he will become convinced, that it is in-
finitely wiser and safer, to form a constitution of our own
in a cool deliberate manner, while we have it in our power,
than to trust such an interesting event to time and chance.
If we omit it now, some *Massenello may hereafter arise,
who laying hold of popular disquietudes, may collect
together the desperate and the discontented, and by

---

* Thomas Anello, otherwise Massenello, a fisherman of Naples,
who after spiriting up his countrymen in the public market place,
against the oppression of the Spaniards, to whom the place was
then subject, prompted them to revolt, and in the space of a day
became King.

assuming to themselves the powers of government, may sweep away the liberties of the continent like a deluge. Should the government of America return again into the hands of Britain, the tottering situation of things, will be a temptation for some desperate adventurer to try his fortune; and in such a case, what relief can Britain give? Ere she could hear the news the fatal business might be done, and ourselves suffering like the wretched Britons under the oppression of the Conqueror. Ye that oppose independance now, ye know not what ye do; ye are opening a door to eternal tyranny, by keeping vacant the seat of government. There are thousands and tens of thousands, who would think it glorious to expel from the continent, that barbarous and hellish power, which hath stirred up the Indians and Negroes to destroy us; the cruelty hath a double guilt, it is dealing brutally by us, and treacherously by them.

To talk of friendship with those in whom our reason forbids us to have faith, and our affections wounded through a thousand pores instruct us to detest, is madness and folly. Every day wears out the little remains of kindred between us and them, and can there be any reason to hope, that as the relationship expires, the affection will increase, or that we shall agree better, when we have ten times more and greater concerns to quarrel over than ever?

Ye that tell us of harmony and reconciliation, can ye restore to us the time that is past? Can ye give to prostitution its former innocence? Neither can ye reconcile Britain and America. The last cord now is broken, the people of England are presenting addresses against us. There are injuries which nature cannot forgive; she would cease to be nature if she did. As well can the lover forgive the ravisher of his mistress, as the continent forgive the murders of Britain. The Almighty hath implanted in us these unextinguishable feelings for good and wise purposes.

They are the guardians of his image in our hearts. They distinguish us from the herd of common animals. The social compact would dissolve, and justice be extirpated the earth, or have only a casual existence were we callous to the touches of affection. The robber and the murderer, would often escape unpunished, did not the injuries which our tempers sustain, provoke us into justice.

O ye that love mankind! Ye that dare oppose, not only the tyranny, but the tyrant, stand forth! Every spot of the old world is over-run with oppression. Freedom hath been hunted round the globe. Asia, and Africa, have long expelled her. – Europe regards her like a stranger, and England hath given her warning to depart. O! receive the fugitive, and prepare in time an asylum for mankind.

OF THE PRESENT ABILITY OF AMERICA, WITH SOME MISELLANEOUS REFLEXIONS.

I have never met with a man, either in England or America, who hath not confessed his opinion, that a separation between the countries, would take place one time or other. And there is no instance in which we have shewn less judgment, than in endeavouring to describe, what we call, the ripeness or fitness of the Continent for independance.

As all men allow the measure, and vary only in their opinion of the time, let us, in order to remove mistakes, take a general survey of things and endeavour if possible, to find out the *very* time. But we need not go far, the inquiry ceases at once, for the *time hath found us*. The general concurrence, the glorious union of all things prove the fact.

It is not in numbers but in unity, that our great strength lies; yet our present numbers are sufficient to repel the force of all the world. The Continent hath, at this time, the largest body of armed and disciplined men of any power under Heaven; and is just arrived at that pitch of strength, in which no single colony is able to support itself, and the whole, when united can accomplish the matter, and either more, or, less than this, might be fatal in its effects. Our land force is already sufficient, and as to naval affairs, we cannot be insensible, that Britain would never suffer an American man of war to be built while the continent remained in her hands. Wherefore we should be no forwarder an hundred years hence in that branch, than we are now; but the truth is, we should be less so, because the timber of the country is every day diminishing, and that which will remain at last, will be far off and difficult to procure.

Were the continent crowded with inhabitants, her sufferings under the present circumstances would be intolerable. The more sea port towns we had, the more should we have both to defend and to loose. Our present numbers are so happily proportioned to our wants, that no man need be idle. The diminution of trade affords an army, and the necessities of an army create a new trade.

Debts we have none; and whatever we may contract on this account will serve as a glorious memento of our virtue. Can we but leave posterity with a settled form of government, an independant constitution of its own, the purchase at any price will be cheap. But to expend millions for the sake of getting a few vile acts repealed, and routing the present ministry only, is unworthy the charge, and is using posterity with the utmost cruelty; because it is leaving them the great work to do, and a debt upon their backs, from which they derive no advantage. Such a thought is unworthy a man of honor, and is the true characteristic of a narrow heart and a pedling politician.

The debt we may contract doth not deserve our regard if the work be but accomplished. No nation ought to be without a debt. A national debt is a national bond; and when it bears no interest, is in no case a grievance. Britain is oppressed with a debt of upwards of one hundred and forty millions sterling, for which she pays upwards of four millions interest. And as a compensation for her debt, she has a large navy; America is without a debt, and without a navy; yet for the twentieth part of the English national debt, could have a navy as large again. The navy of England is not worth, at this time, more than three millions and a half sterling.

The first and second editions of this pamphlet were published without the following calculations, which are now given as a proof that the above estimation of the navy is a just one. *See Entic's naval history, intro.* page 56.

The charge of building a ship of each rate, and furnishing her with masts, yards, sails and rigging, together with a proportion of eight months boatswain's and carpenter's sea-stores, as calculated by Mr Burchett, Secretary to the navy.

		£.
For a ship of 100 guns	——	35,553
90	— —	29,886
80	—— ——	23,638
70	——	17,785
60	— —	14,197
50	——	10,606
40	— —	7,558
30	—— ——	5,846
20	——	3,710

And from hence it is easy to sum up the value, or cost rather, of the whole British navy, which in the year 1757,

when it was as its greatest glory co
ships and guns:

Ships.	Guns.	Cost of one.	C
6 —	100 —	35,553 *l.* —	21
12 —	90 —	29,886 —	358,6
12 —	80 —	23,638 —	283,656
43 —	70 —	17,785 —	746,755
35 —	60 —	14,197 —	496,895
40 —	50 —	10,606 —	424,240
45 —	40 —	7,558 —	340,110
58 —	20 —	3,710 —	215,180
85 Sloops, bombs, and fireships, one with another, at		2,000 —	170,000

Cost 3,266,786

Remains for guns, —— 233,214

Total, 3,500,000

No country on the globe is so happily situated, so internally capable of raising a fleet as America. Tar, timber, iron, and cordage are her natural produce. We need go abroad for nothing. Whereas the Dutch, who make large profits by hiring out their ships of war to the Spaniards and Portuguese, are obliged to import most of the materials they use. We ought to view the building a fleet as an article of commerce, it being the natural manufactory of this country. It is the best money we can lay out. A navy when finished is worth more than it cost. And is that nice point in national policy, in which commerce and protection are united. Let us build; if we want them not, we can sell; and by that means replace our paper currency with ready gold and silver.

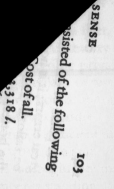

sisted of the following

ost of all.

,318 L.

2

...le in general run into
...one-fourth part should
...Captain Death, stood
...p last war, yet had not
...er complement of men
...w able and social sailors
...ber of active land-men in
...erefore, we never can be
...time matters than now,
...fisheries blocked up, and
...of employ. Men of war of

seventy ... forty years ago in New-England, and why not the same now? Ship-building is America's greatest pride, and in which, she will in time excel the whole world. The great empires of the east are mostly inland, and consequently excluded from the possibility of rivalling her. Africa is in a state of barbarism; and no power in Europe, hath either such an extent of coast, or such an internal supply of materials. Where nature hath given the one, she has withheld the other; to America only hath she been liberal of both. The vast empire of Russia is almost shut out from the sea; wherefore, her boundless forests, her tar, iron, and cordage are only articles of commerce.

In point of safety, ought we to be without a fleet? We are not the little people now, which we were sixty years ago; at that time we might have trusted our property in the streets, or fields rather; and slept securely without locks or bolts to our doors or windows. The case now is altered, and our methods of defence ought to improve with our increase of property. A common pirate, twelve months ago, might have come up the Delaware, and laid the city of Philadelphia under instant contribution, for what sum he pleased; and the same might have happened to other places. Nay, any daring fellow, in a brig of fourteen or sixteen guns, might have robbed the whole Continent, and carried off half a million of money. These are circumstances which demand our attention, and point out the necessity of naval protection.

Some, perhaps, will say, that after we have made it up with Britain, she will protect us. Can we be so unwise as to mean, that she shall keep a navy in our harbours for that purpose? Common sense will tell us, that the power which hath endeavoured to subdue us, is of all others the most improper to defend us. Conquest may be effected under the pretence of friendship; and ourselves, after a long and brave resistance, be at last cheated into slavery. And if her ships are not to be admitted into our harbours, I would ask, how is she to protect us? A navy three or four thousand miles off can be of little use, and on sudden emergencies, none at all. Wherefore, if we must hereafter protect ourselves, why not do it for ourselves? Why do it for another?

The English list of ships of war is long and formidable, but not a tenth part of them are at any one time fit for service, numbers of them not in being; yet their names are pompously continued in the list, if only a plank be left of the ship: and not a fifth part, of such as are fit for service, can be spared on any one station at one time. The East, and West Indies, Mediterranean, Africa, and other parts over which Britain extends her claim, make large demands upon her navy. From a mixture of prejudice and inattention, we have contracted a false notion respecting the navy of England, and have talked as if we should have the whole of it to encounter at once, and for that reason, supposed that we must have one as large; which not being instantly practicable, have been made use of by a set of disguised Tories to discourage our beginning thereon. Nothing can be farther from truth than this; for if America had only a twentieth part of the naval force of Britain, she would be by far an over match for her; because, as we neither have, nor claim any foreign dominion, our whole force would be employed on our own coast, where we should, in the long run, have two to one the advantage of those who had three or four thousand miles to sail over, before they could attack us, and the same distance to return in order to refit and recruit. And although Britain by her fleet, hath a check over our trade to Europe, we have as large a one over her trade to the West-Indies, which, by laying in the neighbourhood of the Continent, is entirely at its mercy.

Some method might be fallen on to keep up a naval force in time of peace, if we should not judge it necessary to support a constant navy. If premiums were to be given to merchants, to build and employ in their service, ships mounted with twenty, thirty, forty, or fifty guns, (the premiums to be in proportion to the loss of bulk to the merchants) fifty or sixty of those ships, with a few guard ships on constant duty, would keep up a sufficient navy, and that without burdening ourselves with the evil so loudly complained of in England, of suffering their fleet, in time of peace to lie rotting in the docks. To unite the sinews of commerce and defence is sound policy; for when our strength and our riches, play into each other's hand, we need fear no external enemy.

In almost every article of defence we abound. Hemp flourishes even to rankness, so that we need not want cordage. Our iron is superior to that of other countries. Our small arms equal to any in the world. Cannon we can cast at pleasure. Saltpetre and gunpowder we are every day producing. Our knowledge is hourly improving. Resolution is our inherent character, and courage hath never yet forsaken us. Wherefore, what is it that we want? Why is it that we hesitate? From Britain we can expect nothing but ruin. If she is once admitted to the government of America again, this Continent will not be worth living in. Jealousies

will be always arising; insurrections will be constantly
happening; and who will go forth to quell them? Who will
venture his life to reduce his own countrymen to a foreign
obedience? The difference between Pennsylvania and
Connecticut, respecting some unlocated lands, shews the
insignificance of a B—sh government, and fully proves,
that nothing but Continental authority can regulate
Continental matters.

Another reason why the present time is preferable to all
others, is, that the fewer our numbers are, the more land
there is yet unoccupied, which instead of being lavished by
the k— on his worthless dependants, may be hereafter
applied, not only to the discharge of the present debt, but
to the constant support of government. No nation under
heaven hath such an advantage as this.

The infant state of the Colonies, as it is called, so far
from being against, is an argument in favor of independance. We are sufficiently numerous, and were we more so,
we might be less united. It is a matter worthy of observa-
tion, that the more a country is peopled, the smaller their
armies are. In military numbers, the ancients far exceeded
the moderns: and the reason is evident, for trade being the
consequence of population, men become too much
absorbed thereby to attend to any thing else. Commerce
diminishes the spirit, both of patriotism and military
defence. And history sufficiently informs us, that the
bravest atchievements were always accomplished in the
non-age of a nation. With the increase of commerce,
England hath lost its spirit. The city of London, notwithstanding its numbers, submits to continued insults with the
patience of a coward. The more men have to lose, the less
willing are they to venture. The rich are in general slaves to
fear, and submit to courtly power with the trembling
duplicity of a spaniel.

Youth is the seed time of good habits, as well in nations

as in individuals. It might be difficult, if not impossible, to form the Continent into one government half a century hence. The vast variety of interests, occasioned by an increase of trade and population, would create confusion. Colony would be against colony. Each being able might scorn each other's assistance: and while the proud and foolish gloried in their little distinctions, the wise would lament that the union had not been formed before. Wherefore, the *present time* is the *true time* for establishing it. The intimacy which is contracted in infancy, and the friendship which is formed in misfortune, are, of all others, the most lasting and unalterable. Our present union is marked with both these characters: we are young, and we have been distressed; but our concord hath withstood our troubles, and fixes a memorable æra for posterity to glory in.

The present time, likewise, is that peculiar time, which never happens to a nation but once, *viz.* the time of forming itself into a government. Most nations have let slip the opportunity, and by that means have been compelled to receive laws from their conquerors, instead of making laws for themselves. First, they had a king, and then a form of government; whereas, the articles or charter of government, should be formed first, and men delegated to execute them afterward: but from the errors of other nations, let us learn wisdom, and lay hold of the present opportunity – *To begin government at the right end.*

When William the conqueror subdued England he gave them law at the point of the sword; and until we consent that the seat of government in America, be legally and authoritatively occupied, we shall be in danger of having it filled by some fortunate ruffian, who may treat us in the same manner, and then, where will be our freedom? where our property?

As to religion, I hold it to be the indispensible duty of all government, to protect all conscientious professors thereof, and I know of no other business which government hath to do therewith. Let a man throw aside that narrowness of soul, that selfishness of principle, which the niggards of all professions are so unwilling to part with, and he will be at once delivered of his fears on that head. Suspicion is the companion of mean souls, and the bane of all good society. For myself I fully and conscientiously believe, that it is the will of the Almighty, that there should be diversity of religious opinions among us: It affords a larger field for our christian kindness. Were we all of one way of thinking, our religious dispositions would want matter for probation; and on this liberal principle, I look on the various denominations among us, to be like children of the same family, differing only, in what is called their Christian names.

In page fifty-four,* I threw out a few thoughts on the propriety of a Continental Charter, (for I only presume to offer hints, not plans) and in this place, I take the liberty of rementioning the subject, by observing, that a charter is to be understood as a bond of solemn obligation, which the whole enters into, to support the right of every separate part, whether of religion, personal freedom, or property, A firm bargain and a right reckoning make long friends.

In a former page I likewise mentioned the necessity of a large and equal representation; and there is no political matter which more deserves our attention. A small number of electors, or a small number of representatives, are equally dangerous. But if the number of the representatives be not only small, but unequal, the danger is increased. As an instance of this, I mention the following; when the Associators petition was before the House of Assembly of Pennsylvania; twenty-eight members only were present, all the Bucks county members, being eight, voted against it, and had seven of the Chester members done the same, this whole province had been governed by two counties only,

* [Page 97 in this edition.]

and this danger it is always exposed to. The unwarrantable stretch likewise, which that house made in their last sitting, to gain an undue authority over the Delegates of that province, ought to warn the people at large, how they trust power out of their own hands. A set of instructions for the Delegates were put together, which in point of sense and business would have dis-honored a school-boy, and after being approved by a *few*, a *very few* without doors, were carried into the House, and there passed *in behalf of the whole colony*; whereas, did the whole colony know, with what ill-will that House hath entered on some necessary public measures, they would not hesitate a moment to think them unworthy of such a trust.

Immediate necessity makes many things convenient, which if continued would grow into oppressions. Expedience and right are different things. When the calamities of America required a consultation, there was no method so ready, or at that time so proper, as to appoint persons from the several Houses of Assembly for that purpose and the wisdom with which they have proceeded hath preserved this continent from ruin. But as it is more than probable that we shall never be without a CONGRESS, every well wisher to good order, must own, that the mode for choosing members of that body, deserves consideration. And I put it as a question to those, who make a study of mankind, whether *representation and election* is not too great a power for one and the same body of men to possess? When we are planning for posterity, we ought to remember that virtue is not hereditary.

It is from our enemies that we often gain excellent maxims, and are frequently surprised into reason by their mistakes. Mr Cornwall (one of the Lords of the Treasury) treated the petition of the New-York Assembly with contempt, because *that* House, he said, consisted but of twenty-six members, which trifling number, he argued, could not with decency be put for the whole. We thank him for his involuntary honesty*.

To Conclude, however strange it may appear to some, or however unwilling they may be to think so, matters not, but many strong and striking reasons may be given, to shew, that nothing can settle our affairs so expeditiously as an open and determined declaration for independance. Some of which are,

First. – It is the custom of nations, when any two are at war, for some other powers, not engaged in the quarrel, to step in as mediators, and bring about the preliminaries of a peace: but while America calls herself the subject of Great Britain, no power, however well disposed she may be, can offer her mediation. Wherefore, in our present state we may quarrel on for ever.

Secondly. – It is unreasonable to suppose, that France or Spain will give us any kind of assistance, if we mean only to make use of that assistance for the purpose of repairing the breach, and strengthening the connection between Britain and America; because, those powers would be sufferers by the consequences.

Thirdly. – While we profess ourselves the subjects of Britain, we must, in the eye of foreign nations, be considered as rebels. The precedent is somewhat dangerous to *their peace*, for men to be in arms under the name of subjects; we on the spot, can solve the paradox: but to unite resistance and subjection, requires an idea much too refined for common understanding.

Fourthly. – Were a manifesto to be published, and despatched to foreign courts, setting forth the miseries we have endured, and the peaceable methods we have

* Those who would fully understand of what great consequence a large and equal representation is to a state, should read Burgh's political Disquisitions.

ineffectually used for redress; declaring, at the same time, that not being able, any longer to live happily or safely under the cruel disposition of the B—sh court, we had been driven to the necessity of breaking off all connection with her; at the same time assuring all such courts of our peaceable disposition towards them, and of our desire of entering into trade with them: Such a memorial would produce more good effects to this Continent, than if a ship were freighted with petitions to Britain.

Under our present denomination of British subjects we can neither be received nor heard abroad: The custom of all courts is against us, and will be so, until, by an independance, we take rank with other nations.

These proceedings may at first appear strange and difficult; but, like all other steps which we have already passed over, will in a little time become familiar and agreeable; and, until an independance is declared, the Continent will feel itself like a man who continues putting off some unpleasant business from day to day, yet knows it must be done, hates to set about it, wishes it over, and is continually haunted with the thoughts of its necessity.

Since the publication of the first edition of this pamphlet, or rather, on the same day on which it came out, the —'s Speech made its appearance in this city. Had the spirit of prophecy directed the birth of this production, it could not have brought it forth, at a more seasonable juncture, or a more necessary time. The bloody mindedness of the one, shew the necessity of pursuing the doctrine of the other. Men read by way of revenge. And the speech instead of terrifying, prepared a way for the manly principles of Independance.

Ceremony, and even, silence, from whatever motive they may arise, have a hurtful tendency, when they give the least degree of countenance to base and wicked performances; wherefore, if this maxim be admitted, it naturally follows, that the —'s speech, as being a piece of finished villainy, deserved, and still deserves, a general execration both by the Congress and the people. Yet as the domestic tranquility of a nation, depends greatly on the *chastity* of what may properly be called NATIONAL MATTERS, it is often better, to pass some things over in silent disdain, than to make use of such new methods of dislike, as might introduce the least innovation, on that guardian of our peace and safety. And perhaps, it is chiefly owing to this prudent delicacy, that the —'s Speech, hath not before now, suffered a public execution. The Speech if it may be called one, is nothing better than a wilful audacious libel against the truth, the common good, and the existence of mankind; and is a formal and pompous method of offering up human sacrifices to the pride of tyrants. But this general massacre of mankind, is one of the privileges, and the certain consequences of K—s; for as nature knows them *not,* they know *not her,* and although they are beings of our *own* creating, they know not *us,* and are become the gods of their creators. The speech hath one good quality, which is, that it is not calculated to deceive, neither can we, even if we would, be deceived by it. Brutality and tyranny appear on the face of it. It leaves us at no loss: And every line convinces, even in the moment of reading, that He, who hunts the woods for prey, the naked and untutored Indian, is less a Savage than the — of B—.

Sir J—n D—e, the putative father of a whining jesuitical piece, fallaciously called, 'The Address of the people of ENGLAND *to the inhabitants of* AMERICA,' hath, perhaps from a vain supposition, that the people *here* were to be frightened at the pomp and description of a king, given, (though very unwisely on his part) the real character of the present one: 'But,' says this writer, 'if you are inclined to pay compliments to an administration, which we do not complain of,' (meaning the Marquis of Rockingham's at the repeal of the Stamp Act) 'it is very unfair in you to withold them from that prince, *by whose* NOD ALONE *they were permitted to do any thing.*' this is toryism with a witness! Here is idolatry even without a mask: And he who can calmly hear, and digest such doctrine, hath forfeited his claim to rationality – an apostate from the order of manhood; and ought to be considered – as one, who hath, not only given up the proper dignity of a man, but sunk himself beneath the rank of animals, and contemptibly crawl through the world like a worm.

However, it matters very little now, what the — of E— either says or does; he hath wickedly broken through every moral and human obligation, trampled nature and conscience beneath his feet; and by a steady and constitutional spirit of insolence and cruelty, procured for himself an universal hatred. It is *now* the interest of America to provide for herself. She hath already a large and young family, whom it is more her duty to take care of, than to be granting away her property, to support a power who is become a reproach to the names of men and christians – YE, whose office it is to watch over the morals of a nation, of whatsoever sect or denomination ye are of, as well as ye, who are more immediately the guardians of the public liberty, if ye wish to preserve your native country uncontaminated by European corruption, ye must in secret wish a separation – But leaving the moral part to private reflection, I shall chiefly confine my farther remarks to the following heads.

First, That it is the interest of America to be separated from Britain.

Secondly. Which is the easiest and most practicable plan, RECONCILIATION or INDEPENDANCE? with some occasional remarks.

In support of the first, I could, if I judged it proper, produce the opinion of some of the ablest and most experienced men on this continent; and whose sentiments, on that head, are not yet publickly known. It is in reality a self-evident position: For no nation in a state of foreign dependance, limited in its commerce, and cramped and fettered in its legislative powers, can ever arrive at any material eminence. America doth not yet know what opulence is; and although the progress which she hath made stands unparalleled in the history of other nations, it is but childhood, compared with what she would be capable of arriving at, had she, as she ought to have, the legislative powers in her own hands. England is, at this time, proudly coveting what would do her no good, were she to accomplish it; and the Continent hesitating on a matter, which will be her final ruin if neglected. It is the commerce and not the conquest of America, by which England is to be benefited, and that would in a great measure continue, were the countries as independant of each other as France and Spain; because in many articles, neither can go to a better market.

But it is the independance of this country on Britain or any other, which is now the main and only object worthy of contention, and which, like all other truths discovered by necessity, will appear clearer and stronger every day.

First. Because it will come to that one time or other.

Secondly. Because the longer it is delayed the harder it will be to accomplish.

I have frequently amused myself both in public and private companies, with silently remarking the spacious errors of those who speak without reflecting. And among the many which I have heard, the following seems the most general, viz. that had this rupture happened forty or fifty years hence, instead of *now*, the Continent would have been more able to have shaken off the dependance. To which I reply, that our military ability *at this time*, arises from the experience gained in the last war, and which in forty or fifty years time, would have been totally extinct. The Continent, would not, by that time, have had a General, or even a military officer left; and we, or those who may succeed us, would have been as ignorant of martial matters as the ancient Indians: And this single position, closely attended to, will unanswerably prove, that the present time is preferable to all others: The argument turns thus – at the conclusion of the last war, we had experience, but wanted numbers; and forty or fifty years hence, we should have numbers, without experience; wherefore, the proper point of time, must be some particular point between the two extremes, in which a sufficiency of the former remains, and a proper increase of the latter is obtained: And that point of time is the present time.

The reader will pardon this digression, as it does not properly come under the head I first set out with, and to which I again return by the following position, viz.

Should affairs be patched up with Britain, and she to remain the governing and sovereign power of America, (which as matters are now circumstanced, is giving up the point entirely) we shall deprive ourselves of the very means of sinking the debt we have or may contract. The value of the back lands which some of the provinces are clandestinely deprived of, by the unjust extention of the limits of Canada, valued only at five pounds sterling per hundred acres, amount to upwards of twenty-five millions, Pennsylvania currency; and the quit-rents at one penny sterling per acre, to two millions yearly.

It is by the sale of those lands that the debt may be sunk, without burthen to any, and the quit-rent reserved thereon, will always lessen, and in time, will wholly support the yearly expence of government. It matters not how long the debt is in paying, so that the lands when sold be applied to the discharge of it, and for the execution of which, the Congress for the time being, will be the continental trustees.

I proceed now to the second head, viz. Which is the earliest and most practicable plan, RECONCILIATION or INDEPENDANCE? with some occasional remarks.

He who takes nature for his guide is not easily beaten out of his argment, and on that ground, I answer *generally* – *That* INDEPENDANCE *being a* SINGLE SIMPLE LINE, *contained within ourselves; and reconciliation, a matter exceedingly perplexed and complicated, and in which, a treacherous capricious court is to interfere, gives the answer without a doubt.*

The present state of America is truly alarming to every man who is capable of reflexion. Without law, without government, without any other mode of power than what is founded on, and granted by courtesy. Held together by an unexampled concurrence of sentiment, which is nevertheless subject to change, and which every secret enemy is endeavouring to dissolve. Our present condition, is, Legislation without law; wisdom without a plan; a constitution without a name; and, what is strangely astonishing, perfect Independance contending for Dependance. The instance is without a precedent; the case never existed before; and who can tell what may be the event? The property of no man is secure in the present unbraced system of things. The mind of the multitude is left at random, and feeling no fixed object before them, they pursue such as fancy or opinion starts. Nothing is criminal; there is no such thing as treason; wherefore, every one thinks himself at liberty to act as he pleases. The Tories dared not to have assembled offensively, had they known that their lives, by that act were forfeited to the laws of the state. A line of distinction should be drawn, between English soldiers taken in battle, and inhabitants of America taken in arms. The first are prisoners, but the latter traitors. The one forfeits his liberty the other his head.

Notwithstanding our wisdom, there is a visible feebleness in some of our proceedings which gives encouragement to dissentions. The Continental belt is too loosely buckled. And if something is not done in time, it will be too late to do any thing, and we shall fall into a state, in which, neither *reconciliation* nor *independance* will be practicable. The — and his worthless adherents are got at their old game of dividing the Continent, and there are not wanting among us, Printers, who will be busy spreading specious falsehoods. The artful and hypocritical letter which appeared a few months ago in two of the New-York papers, and likewise in two others, is an evidence that there are men who want either judgement or honesty.

It is easy getting into holes and corners and talking of reconciliation: But do such men seriously consider, how difficult the|task is, and how dangerous it may prove, should the Continent divide thereon. Do they take within their view, all the various orders of men whose situation and circumstances, as well as their own, are to be considered therein. Do they put themselves in the place of the sufferer whose *all* is *already* gone, and of the soldier, who hath quitted *all* for the defence of his country. If their ill-judged moderation be suited to their own private situations *only*, regardless of others, the event will convince them, that 'they are reckoning without their Host.'

Put us, says some, on the footing we were on in sixty-three: To which I answer, the request is not *now* in the power of Britain to comply with, neither will she propose it; but if it were, and even should be granted, I ask, as a reasonable question, By what means is such a corrupt and faithless court to be kept to its engagements? Another parliament, nay, even the present, may hereafter repeal the obligation, on the pretence of its being violently obtained, or unwisely granted; and in that case, Where is our redress? – No going to law with nations; cannon are the barristers of crowns; and the sword, not of justice, but of war, decides the suit. To be on the footing of sixty-three, it is not sufficient, that the laws only be put on the same state, but, that our circumstances, likewise, be put on the same state; our burnt and destroyed towns repaired or built up, our private losses made good, our public debts (contracted for defence) discharged; otherwise, we shall be millions worse than we were at that enviable period. Such a request had it been complied with a year ago, would have won the heart and soul of the Continent – but now it is too late, 'The Rubicon is passed.'

Besides the taking up arms, merely to enforce the repeal of a pecuniary law, seems as unwarrantable by the divine law, and as repugnant to human feelings, as the taking up arms to enforce obedience thereto. The object, on either side, doth not justify the ways and means; for the lives of men are too valuable to be cast away on such trifles. It is the violence which is done and threatened to our persons; the destruction of our property by an armed force; the invasion of our country by fire and sword, which conscientiously qualifies the use of arms: And the instant, in which such a mode of defence became necessary, all subjection to Britain ought to have ceased; and the independancy of America should have been considered, as dating its æra from, and published by, *the first musket that was fired against her*. This line is a line of consistency; neither drawn by caprice, nor extended by ambition; but produced by a chain of events, of which the colonies were not the authors.

I shall conclude these remarks, with the following timely and well intended hints, We ought to reflect, that there are three different ways by which an independancy may hereafter be effected; and that *one* of those *three,* will one day or other, be the fate of America, viz. By the legal voice of the people in Congress; by a military power; or by a mob: It may not always happen that our soldiers are citizens, and the multitude a body of reasonable men; virtue, as I have already remarked, is not hereditary, neither is it perpetual. Should an independancy be brought about by the first of those means, we have every opportunity and every encouragement before us, to form the noblest, purest constitution on the face of the earth. We have it in our power to begin the world over again. A situation, similar to the present, hath not happened since the days of Noah until now. The birth-day of a new world is at hand, and a race of men perhaps as numerous as all Europe contains, are to receive their portion of freedom from the event of a few months. The Reflexion is awful – and in this point of view, How trifling, how ridiculous, do the little, paltry cavellings, of a few weak or interested men appear, when weighed against the business of a world.

Should we neglect the present favorable and inviting period, and an independance be hereafter effected by any other means, we must charge the consequence to ourselves, or to those rather, whose narrow and prejudiced souls, are habitually opposing the measure, without either inquiring or reflecting. There are reasons to be given in support of Independance, which men should rather privately think of, than be publicly told of. We ought not now to be debating whether we shall be independant or not, but, anxious to accomplish it on a firm, secure, and honorable basis, and uneasy rather that it is not yet began upon. Every day convinces us of its necessity. Even the Tories (if such beings yet remain among us) should, of all men, be the most solicitous to promote it; for, as the appointment of committees at first, protected them from popular rage, so, a wise and well established form of government, will be the only certain means of continuing it securely to them. *Wherefore*, if they have not virtue enough to be WHIGS, they ought to have prudence enough to wish for Independance.

In short, Independance is the only BOND that can tye and keep us together. We shall then see our object, and our ears will be legally shut against the schemes of an intriguing, as well as a cruel enemy. We shall then too, be on a proper footing, to treat with Britain; for there is reason to conclude, that the pride of that court, will be less hurt by treating with the American states for terms of peace, than with those, whom she denominates, 'rebellious subjects,' for terms of accommodation. It is our delaying it that encourages her to hope for conquest, and our backwardness tends only to prolong the war. As we have, without any good effect therefrom, with-held our trade to obtain a redress of our grievances, let us *now* try the alternative, by *independantly* redressing them ourselves, and then offering to open the trade. The mercantile and reasonable part of England will be still with us; because, peace *with* trade, is preferable to war *without* it. And if this offer be not accepted, other courts may be applied to.

On these grounds I rest the matter. And as no offer hath

yet been made to refute the doctrine contained in the former editions of this pamphlet, it is a negative proof, that either the doctrine cannot be refuted, or, that the party in favour of it are too numerous to be opposed. WHEREFORE, instead of gazing at each other with suspicious or doubtful curiosity, let each of us, hold out to his neighbour the hearty hand of friendship, and unite in drawing a line, which, like an act of oblivion, shall bury in forgetfulness every former dissention. Let the names of Whig and Tory be extinct; and let none other be heard among us, than those of *a good citizen, an open and resolute friend, and a virtuous supporter of the* RIGHTS *of* MANKIND *and of the* FREE AND INDEPENDANT STATES OF AMERICA.

*

To the Representatives of the Religious Society of the People called Quakers, or to so many of them as were concerned in publishing a late piece, entitled 'The Ancient Testimony and 'Principles of the people called Quakers renewed, with respect to 'the King and Government, and Touching the Commotions now 'prevailing in these and other parts of America, addressed to the 'people in general.'

THE Writer of this, is one of those few, who never dishonors religion either by ridiculing, or cavilling at any denomination whatsoever. To God, and not to man, are all men accountable on the score of religion. Wherefore, this epistle is not so properly addressed to you as a religious, but as a political body, dabbling in matters, which the professed Quietude of your Principles instruct you not to meddle with.

As you have, without a proper authority for so doing,

put yourselves in the place of the whole body of the Quakers, so, the writer of this, in order to be on an equal rank with yourselves, is under the necessity, of putting himself in the place of all those who approve the very writings and principles, against which your testimony is directed: And he hath chosen their singular situation, in order that you might discover in him, that presumption of character which you cannot see in yourselves. For neither he nor you have any claim or title to *Political Representation*.

When men have departed from the right way, it is no wonder that they stumble and fall. And it is evident from the manner in which ye have managed your testimony, that politics, (as a religious body of men) is not your proper Walk; for however well adapted it might appear to you, it is, nevertheless, a jumble of good and bad put unwisely together, and the conclusion drawn therefrom, both unnatural and unjust.

The two first pages, (and the whole doth not make four) we give you credit for, and expect the same civility from you, because the love and desire of peace is not confined to Quakerism, it is the *natural*, as well as the religious wish of all denominations of men. And on this ground, as men labouring to establish an Independant Constitution of our own, do we exceed all others in our hope, end, and aim. *Our plan is peace for ever.* We are tired of contention with Britain, and can see no real end to it but in a final separation. We act consistently, because for the sake of introducing an endless and uninterrupted peace, do we bear the evils and burthens of the present day. We are endeavouring, and will steadily continue to endeavor, to separate and dissolve a connexion which hath already filled our land with blood; and which, while the name of it remains, will be the fatal cause of future mischiefs to both countries.

We fight neither for revenge nor conquest; neither from

pride nor passion; we are not insulting the world with our fleets and armies, nor ravaging the globe for plunder. Beneath the shade of our own vines are we attacked; in our own houses, and on our own lands, is the violence committed against us. We view our enemies in the characters of Highwaymen and Housebreakers, and having no defence for ourselves in the civil law, are obliged to punish them by the military one, and apply the sword, in the very case, where you have before now, applied the halter.—Perhaps we feel for the ruined and insulted sufferers in all and every part of the continent, and with a degree of tenderness which hath not yet made its way into some of your bosoms. But be ye sure that ye mistake not the cause and ground of your Testimony. Call not coldness of soul, religion; nor put the *Bigot* in the place of the *Christian*.

O ye partial ministers of your own acknowledged principles. If the bearing arms be sinful, the first going to war must be more so, by all the difference between wilful attack and unavoidable defence. Wherefore, if ye really preach from conscience, and mean not to make a political hobby-horse of your religion, convince the world thereof, by proclaiming your doctrine to our enemies, *for they likewise bear* ARMS. Give us proof of your sincerity by publishing it at St. James's, to the commanders in chief at Boston, to the Admirals and Captains who are piratically ravaging our coasts, and to all the murdering miscreants who are acting in authority under HIM whom ye profess to serve. Had ye the honest soul of **Barclay* ye would

* 'Thou hast tasted of prosperity and adversity; thou knowest 'what it is to be banished thy native country, to be over-ruled as 'well as to rule, and set upon the throne; and being *oppressed*.thou 'hast reason to know now *hateful* the *oppressor* is both to God and 'man: If after all these warnings and advertisements, thou dost not 'turn unto the Lord with all thy heart, but forget him who remem-'bered thee in thy distress, and give up thyself to follow lust and 'vanity, surely great will be thy condemnation.—Against which

preach repentance to *your* king; Ye would tell the Royal — his sins, and warn him of eternal ruin. Ye would not spend your partial invectives against the injured and the insulted only, but like faithful ministers, would cry aloud and *spare none*. Say not that ye are persecuted, neither endeavour to make us the authors of that reproach, which, ye are bringing upon yourselves; for we testify unto all men, that we do not complain against you because ye are *Quakers*, but because ye pretend to *be* and are NOT Quakers.

Alas! it seems by the particular tendency of some part of your testimony, and other parts of your conduct, as if all sin was reduced to, and comprehended in *the act of bearing arms*, and that by the *people only*. Ye appear to us, to have mistaken party for conscience, because the general tenor of your actions wants uniformity: And it is exceedingly difficult to us to give credit to many of your pretended scruples; because we see them made by the same men, who, in the very instant that they are exclaiming against the mammon of this world, are nevertheless, hunting after it with a step as steady as Time, and an appetite as keen as Death.

The quotation which ye have made from Proverbs, in the third page of your testimony, that, 'when a man's ways please the Lord, he maketh even his enemies to be at peace with him'; is very unwisely chosen on your part; because it amounts to a proof, that the king's ways (whom ye are so desirous of supporting) do *not* please the Lord, otherwise, his reign would be in peace.

I now proceed to the latter part of your testimony, and

'snare, as well as the temptation of those who may or do feed thee, 'and prompt thee to evil, the most excellent and prevalent remedy 'will be, to apply thyself to that light of Christ which shineth in thy 'conscience and which neither can, nor will flatter thee, nor suffer 'thee to be at ease in thy sins.'

Barclay's Address to Charles II.

that, for which all the foregoing seems only an introduction, viz.

'It hath ever been our judgment and principle, since we 'were called to profess the light of Christ Jesus, mani- 'fested in our consciences unto this day, that the setting up 'and putting down kings and governments, is God's 'peculiar prerogative; for causes best known to himself: 'And that it is not our business to have any hand or 'contrivance therein; nor to be busy bodies above our 'station, much less to plot and contrive the ruin, or over- 'turn any of them, but to pray for the king, and safety of 'our nation, and good of all men: That we may live a 'peaceable and quiet life, in all goodliness and honesty; 'under the government which God is pleased to set over us.' — If these are *really* your principles why do ye not abide by them? Why do ye not leave that, which ye call God's Work, to be managed by himself? These very principles instruct you to wait with patience and humility, for the event of all public measures, and to receive *that event* as the divine will towards you. *Wherefore*, what occasion is there for your *political testimony* if you fully believe what it contains? And the very publishing it proves, that either, ye do not believe what ye profess, or have not virtue enough to practise what ye believe.

The principles of Quakerism have a direct tendency to make a man the quiet and inoffensive subject of any, and every government *which is set over him*. And if the setting up and putting down of kings and governments is God's peculiar prerogative, he most certainly will not be robbed thereof by us; wherefore, the principle itself leads you to approve of every thing, which ever happened, or may happen to kings as being his work, OLIVER CROMWELL thanks you. – CHARLES, then, died not by the hands of man; and should the present Proud Imitator of him, come to the same untimely end, the writers and publishers of the

testimony, are bound by the doctrine it contains, to
applaud the fact. Kings are not taken away by miracles,
neither are changes in governments brought about by
any other means than such as are common and human;
and such as we are now using. Even the dispersing of the
Jews, though foretold by our Saviour, was effected by arms.
Wherefore, as ye refuse to be the means on one side, ye
ought not to be meddlers on the other; but to wait the
issue in silence; and unless you can produce divine authority, to prove, that the Almighty who hath created and
placed this *new* world, at the greatest distance it could
possibly stand, east and west, from every part of the old,
doth, nevertheless, disapprove of its being independant
of the corrupt and abandoned court of B—n, unless I say,
ye can show this, how can ye, on the ground of your principles, justify the exciting and stirring up of the people
'firmly to unite in the *abhorrence* of all such *writings*, and
'*measures*, as evidence a desire and design to break off the
'*happy* connexion we have hitherto enjoyed, with the
'kingdom of Great-Britain, and our just and necessary
'subordination to the king, and those who are lawfully
'placed in authority under him.' What a slap in the face is
here! the men, who, in the very paragraph before, have
quietly and passively resigned up the ordering, altering,
and disposal of kings and governments, into the hands of
God, are now recalling their principles, and putting in for
a share of the business. Is it possible, that the conclusion,
which is here justly quoted, can any ways follow from the
doctrine laid down? The inconsistency is too glaring
not to be seen; the absurdity too great not to be
laughed at; and such as could only have been made
by those, whose understandings were darkened by the
narrow and crabby spirit of a despairing political party;
for ye are not to be considered as the whole body of

the Quakers but only as a factional and fractional part thereof.

Here ends the examination of your testimony; (which I call upon no man to abhor, as ye have done, but only to read and judge of fairly;) to which I subjoin the following remark; 'That the setting up and putting down of kings,' most certainly mean, the making him a king, who is yet not so, and the making him no king who is already one. And pray what hath this to do in the present case? We neither mean to *set up* nor to *put down*, neither to *make* nor to *unmake*, but to have nothing to *do* with them. Wherefore, your testimony in whatever light it is viewed serves ònly to dishonour your judgment, and for many other reasons had better have been let alone than published.

First. Because it tends to the decrease and reproach of all religion whatever, and is of the utmost danger to society, to make it a party in political disputes.

Secondly. Because it exhibits a body of men, numbers of whom disavow the publishing political testimonies, as being concerned therein and approvers thereof.

Thirdly. Because it hath a tendency to undo that continental harmony and friendship which yourselves by your late liberal and charitable donations hath lent a hand to establish; and the preservation of which, is of the utmost consequence to us all.

And here without anger or resentment I bid you farewell. Sincerely wishing, that as men and christians, ye may always fully and uninterruptedly enjoy every civil and religious right; and be, in your turn, the means of securing it to others; but that the example which ye have unwisely set, of mingling religion with politics, *may be disavowed and reprabated by every inhabitant of* AMERICA.

FINIS